SEDONA

OFFICIAL GUIDE TO RED ROCK COUNTRY

By Lawrence W. Cheek

Photography by
Arizona Highways Contributors

Second Edition, Second Printing

ARIZONA HIGHWAYS
BOOKS

CONTENTS

These images, also seen in the five chapters of this book, represent a photographic summary. From left: Paradise Found — an overview of red rock country. Inside Sedona — artistic moods flourish. Outside Sedona — terrain suited for active recreation. Day Trips — ancient ruins are on the itinerary. Farther Out — overnighters to the Grand Canyon and elsewhere.

For several years I had one of the best and most implausible jobs in Arizona: Sedona bureau chief for a regional travel magazine. "Best" for obvious reasons; "implausible" because I didn't live anywhere near Sedona. But I had been a frequent visitor since the 1970s, had reported on her growing pains, and loved hiking the red rocks. In fact, I *discovered* hiking out here among these rocks, and they became the proving ground for all my novice faux pas. Happily, it's a forgiving landscape: I'm still alive.

The hard work of writing more articles about Sedona meant, of course, more expeditions to Sedona. More hikes, more interviews with artists and other engaging characters, more encounters with the prehistoric culture that left its remnants around the rocks. And Sedona transformed me.

I used to love big cities, the hubbub of their architecture and their concentration of flesh and ideas. I liked nature in the abstraction. I could easily negotiate a European subway system, but not the wilderness trails of my home state. The red rocks changed all that — reversed it, in fact. Nature towers over Sedona, demanding our respect and attention, offering to instruct and fulfill. For proper instruction I found I had to get out there, touch it physically and feel it spiritually, and occasionally let it beat me up a bit. And I fell in love.

My friend Mike Bower, a Sedona architect with a fierce lion's commitment to environmental preservation, once put it this way: "Sedona's role in the world is one of celebration of nature, spirit, humanity, and man's relationship to the Earth." I once joined another acquaintance, a Havasupai Indian named Uqualla, on a canyon hike near Sedona. "The rocks and trees are living essences," he said. "They have the ability to communicate to us — if only we listen."

That's what this book is about: listening. Sedona calls to us in various ways, and we respond by turning to art, science, meditation or environmental activism. We may become photographers, hiking enthusiasts, or . . . residents of Sedona. There is only one constant: No one who comes here is ever the same again.

— Lawrence W. Cheek

Lawrence W. Cheek lived in Tucson for 23 years, where he worked as a newspaper reporter, magazine editor, and freelance writer. He now lives in the Cascade foothills near Seattle, but commutes regularly to his native Southwest to work on magazine articles and books. He has written seven books for Arizona Highways.

SEDONA: OFFICIAL GUIDE TO
RED ROCK COUNTRY

Originally published in 1999 as *Sedona Calling: A Guide to Red Rock Country.*

Revised and reformatted for second edition, 2003. Revised for 4th overall printing, 2004.

Printed in Hong Kong

BOOK DESIGNER BARBARA GLYNN DENNEY
PRODUCTION ASSISTANT LINDA LONGMIRE
PHOTOGRAPHY EDITOR RICHARD MAACK
COPY EDITORS STEVE FOX, EVELYN HOWELL, AND PK PERKIN MCMAHON
EDITORIAL INTERN EMILY LYONS
BOOK EDITOR BOB ALBANO

Published by the Book Division of *Arizona Highways* magazine, a monthly publication of the Arizona Department of Transportation 2039 West Lewis Avenue, Phoenix, Arizona 85009. Telephone: (602) 712-2200. Web site: www.arizonahighways.com

Publisher WIN HOLDEN
Managing Editor BOB ALBANO
Associate Editor EVELYN HOWELL
Associate Editor PK PERKIN MCMAHON
Art Director BARBARA GLYNN DENNEY
Photography Director PETER ENSENBERGER
Production Director CINDY MACKEY

Library of Congress Catalog Number 2002115045
ISBN 1932082115

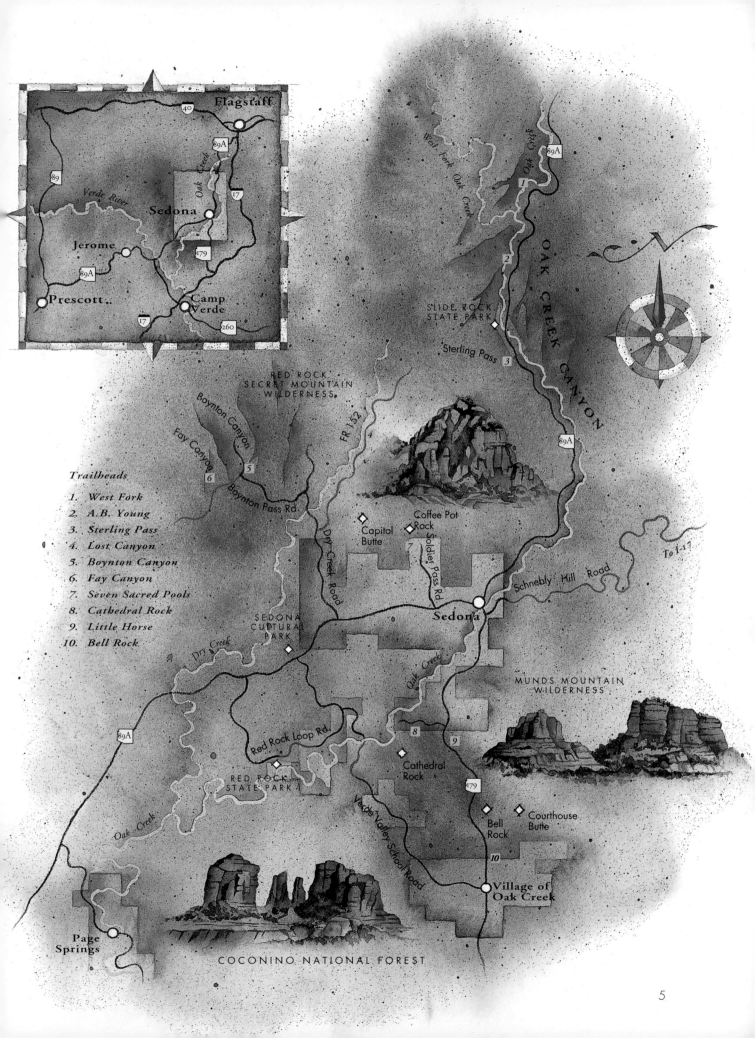

Flagstaff

40

89A

Oak Creek

89

Verde River

17

Sedona

Jerome

179

89A

Prescott

Camp
Verde

17

260

West Fork Oak Creek

Oak Creek

89A

1

OAK CREEK CANYON

2

SLIDE ROCK
STATE PARK

Sterling Pass

3

RED ROCK
SECRET MOUNTAIN
WILDERNESS

Boynton Canyon

Fay Canyon

FR 152

4

89A

5

6

Boynton Pass Rd.

Trailheads

1. *West Fork*
2. *A.B. Young*
3. *Sterling Pass*
4. *Lost Canyon*
5. *Boynton Canyon*
6. *Fay Canyon*
7. *Seven Sacred Pools*
8. *Cathedral Rock*
9. *Little Horse*
10. *Bell Rock*

Capitol
Butte

Coffee Pot
Rock

7

Soldier Pass Rd.

Dry Creek Road

To I-17

Schnebly Hill Road

Sedona

SEDONA
CULTURAL
PARK

Dry Creek

MUNDS MOUNTAIN
WILDERNESS

89A

Red Rock Loop Rd.

Oak Creek

8

9

RED ROCK
STATE PARK

Cathedral
Rock

179

Verde Valley School Road

Bell
Rock

Courthouse
Butte

10

Oak Creek

Page
Springs

Village of
Oak Creek

COCONINO NATIONAL FOREST

CHAPTER ONE

Paradise Found

Origins of Red Rock Fever

This very diversity of climate and water supply which made these hills and plains a treasure house of wealth and beauty likewise made them a fragile dwelling for the modern white man. The engines wherewith he conquers these rocks and rills and templed hills are stronger than his understanding of what hills are, and more powerful than his vaunted love for them.

—ALDO LEOPOLD
From the unpublished book,
Southwest Game Fields

Top: A cliff dwelling occupies a niche in Lost Canyon. Larry Lindahl Above: Sugarloaf Mountain, the low mound, and Coffee Pot Rock preside in this view of west Sedona. Bob & Suzanne Clemenz Right: Cathedral Rock overlooks Oak Creek at Red Rock Crossing. George Stocking

They call it Red Rock Fever, and not as a joke. It begins as an eerie electric shiver near the apex of the spine and then migrates upward to the cortex, where it shuts down the Rational Judgment Department and blossoms into an irresistible urge to *drop everything and move here.* This progression often occurs within a few hours, or minutes, of the victim's first sight of Sedona.

A New Jersey couple taking in a wide swath of the West drove into town for a first visit. "Stop the car," said the wife. "This is the place." They located a broker and began looking at lots before they even looked for a motel. "It was almost like the

Right: Globemallow, larkspur, paintbrush, and prickly pear cactus pave the base of Courthouse Rock. Larry Lindahl

impulse just came through me and I wasn't even saying it," she recalls.

A young South African with a degree in urban planning was hitchhiking around the States when he stumbled across Sedona. A quick look around confirmed for him that the town sorely needed urban planning, but since it wasn't yet incorporated, there wasn't much of it going on.

"So I waltzed into one of the Jeep tour companies and said, 'I'm a hell of a tour guide.' " They hired him. Eventually, he became a planner for finally-incorporated Sedona.

I asked a sales clerk in an uptown boutique what had brought her here.

"God," she replied dreamily.

God, however, had not provided a way for her to actually live in Sedona on $6.50 an hour, so she was commuting from Camp Verde, 30 miles away and well out of sight of any red rocks.

"A lot of gallery owners are commuting these days, too," she said. In 2003, the average sale price of a Sedona home was $416,000.

This is heart-stopping, achingly beautiful, ineffably alluring land. It should have been roped off as a national park back around the time of Teddy Roosevelt, saving it from the desultory development that even many resident Sedonans lament today. In a perfect world, no architecture would perturb the

spectacle; no rumble of traffic would diminish the delicate tinkle of Oak Creek. But even with all the development, the power of the place seems little diminished. More than 4 million people come to visit every year, and more than a few of them find a way to stay.

Pretty amazing for a place boasting rust as the prime attraction.

The geology of Sedona looks complicated, but it actually can be explained simply in a few sentences:

Imagine a warm, shallow tropical sea. Sediment filtering through the water becomes the limestone base of the formations on Sedona's skyline today. The sea retreats, sandy desert usurps its place, and then the water laps up again. This cycle, begun 300 million years ago, keeps repeating, leaving limestone and sandstone strata of different colors and textures, which geologists can read in the rocks today. The spectacular spectrum

of buff, orange, salmon, and vermilion in these strata — the Supai group, the Hermit formation and the Schnebly Hill formation — is the product of iron in the sandstone and limestone. When it rains, the iron rusts. The strange shapes of the rocks are due to the fact that each stratum, having a different degree of hardness, yields in a different way to the eroding forces of water, ice, and wind.

Paleontologists (and amateur fossil finders) also like the history of life embedded in the rocks. The Kaibab formation, a remnant of one of the oceans, yields fossils of sponges, crustaceans, and aquatic worms.

Thus goes the science, but the facts hardly explain the effect that this landscape exerts on the human spirit. People experience an emotional reaction to the landforms, the light, and the weather.

The land that cradles Sedona is too botanically luxurious to qualify as a desert — it enjoys an annual average rainfall of 17.15 inches — but it's also too open, too brittle, too aggressive to be forest. Try beating a straight path between any two points in the Sedona outback, and a motley militia of shindagger agave, prickly pear cactus, and catclaw acacia will cheerfully demonstrate its armament. Where rain congregates in the canyons, however, genuine forests do flourish — even if they're just six feet high and composed mainly of manzanita, a strange and beautiful bush-tree with spider limbs and satiny, wine-red bark. Variety is never a problem here; within 10 miles of town you can find seven distinct biological communities, ranging from desert grassland through Verde River riparian to ponderosa pine-fir forest on the overlooks of Oak Creek Canyon.

The red rocks, too, are alive. Not biologically, but, for want of a more tightly defined word, spiritually. They change in color and character every hour. I have seen them in a gray, woolly fog where they seemed to float, like ghostly icebergs cruising the sky. Under a bright midmorning sun, they may be a pale, cool violet; then as the day burns on, they shift into the red and orange regions of the spectrum. Approaching a late summer sunset, thunderclouds will sometimes roll in, turning the sky to charcoal and enveloping the land in ominous shadow. Then

Below: At sunset, the rocks catch fire, and the landscape seems to guard secrets.
George Stocking

there will be a slit in the overcast, and an arrow of amber sunlight will slash through and set one rock dramatically afire. At sunset on clear evenings, the fire colors turn to dying embers and then to rusty nuggets against a violet sky, and the draws and crevices blacken into voids that seem to guard inexpressible secrets.

Even as the rocks continue to cycle through their chameleon moods, they remain immutable fixtures of the landscape. They seem to have existed forever and to be keeping a promise to persevere long after the momentary blight of civilization has passed. Sedona, more than any other place, recalls the English novelist J.B. Priestley's haunting description of Arizona in 1937: "It seemed to me the oldest country I had ever seen, the real antique land, first cousin to the moon."

Or Welsh-born author and outdoorsman Colin Fletcher, in his preface to *The Complete Walker III*: "In the desert you rediscover . . . the cleanness that exists in spite of the dust, the complexity that underlies the apparent openness . . . but above all you rediscover the echoing silence that you had thought you would never forget."

SEDONA WAS FOUNDED IN 1902, a decade before President William Howard Taft, after some grumbling about the populist tilt of the Territory's proposed constitution, signed Arizona into the family of states. Aside from a handful of homesteads in Oak Creek Canyon, the red rock country was wild, remote, and virtually unknown. But so

Previous spread: A winter storm casts a ghostly tone over Steamboat Rock. Randy Prentice
Top: With a little imagination, perhaps you can see why this rock is called Lion and Lioness. Dick Canby
Right: At the top of this Wilson Mountain trail, the hiker will find a fantastic view of Oak Creek Canyon. Mike Padian
Bottom: At 4,500 feet, the Sedona area rarely receives this much snow. The storm dropped five inches, frosting the sandstone cliffs and the piñon of the Soldier Pass area. Bob & Suzanne Clemenz

Left: Pendley Arch, or
Window Rock, lies in
Oak Creek Canyon.
Larry Lindahl
Below: Sterling Pass Trail
leads through a forest.
Larry Lindahl
Bottom: Hiking along
the West Fork of Oak
Creek means getting
your feet wet.
Bob & Suzanne Clemenz

was most of Arizona. Phoenix —
the Territorial capital and, in
the imagination of one
booster, her "commercial
metropolis" — had a population
of 5,500.

Sedona's story begins with
two brothers, T.C. and Ellsworth
Schnebly, who owned a
hardware store in Gorin,
Missouri. Ellsworth decided
to test the Oak Creek area
to see if the dry, mild climate
would improve his health. It
did, and he also fell in love with
the land. The hardware store,
meanwhile, wasn't thriving, so in
1902, T.C., his 25-year-old wife,
and their two children followed,
claiming an 80-acre homestead
on the west bank of Oak Creek.
They built a plain, two-story
wood frame home with, of all
things, a white picket fence,
where Los Abrigados Resort
sprawls today. They planted
orchards, took in overnight
guests, and applied for a post
office permit. T.C. proposed
two names for the settlement,
both of which the postmaster
rejected because they were too
long to fit on a cancellation
stamp. Ellsworth then
suggested naming the
settlement after T.C.'s wife,
Sedona. Let us give thanks.
T.C.'s ideas for a name had
been Oak Creek Crossing
and Schnebly Station.

Sedona Schnebly proved to
be a woman who deserved the
honor. She had been born into a
well-to-do family and had grown
up expecting to lead a life of "big
hats and temperance meetings,"
said her great-granddaughter,
Lisa Schnebly Heidinger, who
lives in Phoenix today. When
Sedona and T.C. left Missouri

for their Arizona adventure, it infuriated Sedona's father to the extent that he slashed her out of his will.

"I think the move shocked the hell out of her," Heidinger said. "But she didn't realize the extent of her own strength. I have a feeling she wanted the adventure, but never knew it until she experienced it. She tested very, very well."

Sedona, the accidental pioneer, learned to tend the orchards and herd cattle, ran a primordial bed-and-breakfast inn, played the piano to entertain guests, killed rattlesnakes with a broom, eventually raised six children, and watched helplessly as one of them died in a tragic accident. Her daughter Pearl was riding a pony when she spotted an Indian potsherd and stopped to pick it up. The pony spooked and bolted, dragging Pearl alongside, her foot caught in the stirrup. Sedona raced after her, but there was no way to stop the battering. Sedona buried her daughter in front of the house, and withdrew into a cocoon of remorse and nightmares.

Still, "She was a forerunner of today's supermoms," Heidinger told me with pride. In her grandma years, the locals came to call her Mother Schnebly, a warm tribute to the supermom of a town.

Visitors can contemplate Sedona Schnebly outside the city's public library today. The bronze sculpture by Susan

An agave stalk stands watch on the western edge of the Red Rock-Secret Mountain Wilderness.
David H. Smith

Kliewer reconstructs her as bold and forthright, and as graceful as possible within the swaddling confines of a Victorian dress. There is also a revealing photo of her in the archives. Her huge, impassive, doe eyes look like bottomless reservoirs of determination. She was not beautiful, but she had the right

Sedona and red rock formations unfold from an overlook along Schnebly Hill Road. George Stocking

stuff to be a pioneer.

The first 50 years were uneventful for Sedona, the town. Oak Creek offered the only available water, and it wasn't enough for large-scale agriculture or development. Government geologists insisted there was no water underground. In 1948, a driller who suspected differently sank a well, and it produced. That primed Sedona for its boom.

Page Stegner, a writer who went to a boarding school

nearby, recalls the Sedona of 1951 as a rustic refueling station offering not much more than cold pop, gas, and cigarettes, the place "where they coined the phrase, 'If you blink, you'll miss it.' "

In an otherwise cranky essay for *Audubon* magazine in 1981, Stegner remembered his happily misspent days in innocent Sedona, "when the sun would bake the valley to a brickyard, and the red dust would powder so fine that it clogged the pores

and formed a little nosebleed rime around the nostrils, (and) I'd scuttle down through the washes like a scorpion shaken out of a hot boot, fling myself into one of the sandstone pools upstream from the ford, and cling there to a root snaggle below the surface until my head would ache behind the eyes from the cold."

When in 1981 Stegner returned for a second look, he didn't much like what he saw — an unincorporated, sprawling town burgeoning in wealth and sophistication and clotting the desert air powder so fine as contractors resculpted the red hills to make flat places for new shops and houses. What chance does this outpost of Eden stand, he wondered, "when one out of every 20 residents is a real estate agent?"

That figure, of course, was gross exaggeration. Still is. In 2002 just one of every 29 residents was a real estate agent.

Most Sedonans today lament the frenzy of the boom and the vacuum of coherent planning in which it occurred. Since Sedona had no town government of its own and it straddled a county line, residents lurched from one county seat to the other in an endless succession of zoning and development fights. The real issue — how to accommodate growth without scarring the scenery that people were coming to see — was too thorny for such a haphazard process to grasp. The opportunity to create a special kind of community was lost. Sedona today has no definable town center, public park, nor

Sedona and T.C. Schnebly pose in 1897, five years before homesteading on Oak Creek. Special Collections Library, Northern Arizona University, Flagstaff

arts district. But there is some good news: after years of study and debate, the City Council has finally decided to proceed with a creekside walk from uptown Sedona to the Tlaquepaque bridge.

Belatedly, planning took root in Sedona in the 1990s. Piece by piece, the newly incorporated city adopted a sign ordinance, a community plan, and architectural design review to try to preserve the scenic views and discourage buildings that leap out of the rocks and clamor for attention. None of this was easy.

"The community started off really polarized," recalled Roger Eastman, a city planner. "But we all had the same goal — to integrate the built forms of the town into the natural forms around us. By the time we were finished, both sides had come around to the middle — a kind of a greening of the developers and a browning of the environmentalists."

Richard V. Dahl, a prominent real estate agent, expressed a sentiment that you didn't hear much in the Sedona

of 20 years back.

"Living here carries with it a responsibility," he told me in a recent conversation. "We live in one of the most treasured sites in the world. It's not our private preserve."

The planning is making some difference. The McDonald's in West Sedona sports teal, not golden, arches. A car wash melts into the red rock background with a low profile and a salmon color scheme. A big three-level motel steps down a hillside like an angular Slinky, instead of presenting a hulking three-story facade to the street. And the walkway along Oak Creek is closer to becoming a reality. At the same time, though, Sedona's increasing wealth has meant the building of bigger and bigger custom homes on prominent hillsides — 5,000 to 10,000 square feet is not uncommon — and nothing in the native repertoire of runt trees grows high enough to hide them.

By 2004, the settlement that almost got named Schnebly Station had grown into a sophisticated city of 10,800 people. Planners expect a "completed" city of about 15,400 by 2020, when Sedona laps up against the last National Forest boundary. Though houses are unaffordable by most working people's standards, there is little sentiment locally for increased housing density or land swaps with the Forest Service.

FALLING FOR THE ROCKS — and the color, the crisp starlight, even the botanical cutlery — is quick and inevitable. It may take

two or three visits to appreciate the quirks and traditions of Sedona's peculiar stew of civilization, but it happens. Where else could you enjoy a white-tablecloth resort breakfast of an orange frittata with a cloud of tomatillo salsa — precisely the colors of the canyon outside — followed by a visit to a psychic who advertises herself as a "multidimensional glitch remover," and then rattle away in a gaily colored Jeep to tour prehistoric ruins and male or female (your choice) vortexes?

For a couple of generations before the boom of the '70s (and the '80s and '90s), Sedona remained a sleepy hangout for a few artists, a sprinkling of midcentury pioneers, and second-home owners enjoying an escape from Phoenix or southern California. People discovered it through word of mouth, travel writers, and exposure on the silver screen.

The movie industry discovered Sedona before the tourists, beginning in 1923 with Victor Fleming's direction of the silent-movie adaptation of Zane Grey's novel, *The Call of the Canyon*. Although for a long time the red rocks were just black and white, the visual drama of wide, open spaces, towering buttes, and exotic chaparral formed a perfect stage set for classic Westerns: Where in North America could a man on a horse gallop around a land more evocative of heroic challenge? (And yet Hollywood still itched to improve it. In the 1950 Jimmy Stewart blockbuster *Broken Arrow*, fake plaster-of-paris saguaros were installed

around the Sedona outback to suggest the iconic West more thoroughly. A saguaro would no sooner grow as a native plant in Sedona than in San Francisco.) After the Western genre burned out, Sedona continued as a backdrop for TV episodes, music videos, commercials, and print ads. The red rocks have helped sell Land Rovers, Kodak film, Lee jeans, Ray-Ban sunglasses, and, for reasons less clear, the services of 1st Alabama Bank.

The 1980s brought international sophistication — high-end restaurants, high-priced art in the galleries, and destination resorts. One resort, Enchantment, actually started out with a dress code — jackets at dinner, "traditional whites" on the tennis courts. Sedona Schnebly, who borrowed T.C.'s overalls for work, would not have understood. (Now under more enlightened management, Enchantment no longer dictates guests' dress.)

The '80s also brought spiritual seekers, mystics, cranks, and fanatics. And especially entrepreneurs. The forms in which they've marketed Sedona's mystique are as fanciful as the red rocks themselves. A few years ago, howling coyotes infested every boutique and gallery, in every conceivable form. Then the icon became Kokopelli, the prehistoric hunchback flute player. Sedona boutiques present him on T-shirts, electric switch plates, earrings, wind chimes, lawn sculptures, napkin holders, and boxes of Indian corn bread mix. The American West sometimes

seems too huge, too deep, and too complicated to grasp unless we repackage it as a cartoon.

Sedona even markets its distinctive dirt — ready to wear. A local fashion company advertises shirts hand-dyed with Sedona Red Dirt — "Famous for its long-lasting properties, (it) has been

blessed and is believed to bring good luck to the wearer."

For obvious reasons, Sedona has become a mecca for well-off retirees. But the median age is now falling, thanks to the fax, the computer, and the Internet. There is a steadily growing community of freelance "consultants" who became allergic to the urban tumult of New York, San Francisco, or Phoenix, and who are now wiring into the world from Sedona.

Ed Southwell is one of the refugees. He didn't exactly catch Red Rock Fever; he just knew he wanted something other than city life.

"We wanted our eight-year-old daughter to have the same

Cathedral Rock dominates the landscape seen from Red Rock Loop Road, west of Sedona.
Larry Lindahl

freedoms we had when we grew up," he said, "such as being able to ride her bike around the block in safety."

Southwell has run his

national market research business from his Sedona home since 1992. It took a while to plug in: when he started, Sedona didn't even have a local AOL phone number.

"But now there's a satellite link, so we've got DSL just like the big boys," he said.

Business is fine, and clients are envious. "They're always trying to come up with reasons to have meetings here. When I'm making a presentation I'll throw in a slide of Sedona, and someone will always say, "Oh, wow, that is such a cool place."

Richard Drayton is another. In the 1980s, he abandoned a prosperous career in Los Angeles to live in Sedona and paint. Then came the digital revolution, and he invented a prosperous commercial art career, creating artwork on the computer and sending it by modem to clients around the country.

"My studio looks more and more like a computer room than an art studio," he said. "I keep a stack of colored pencils on a desk so I can look at them once in a while and remind myself of what I am."

The consequence of all this is that Sedona today is a place of more variety than ever. There's intellectual capital, creative energy, remarkable sophistication, and, with somewhat more effort than it once took, solitude. If you come to hike, more than 100 trails lace the surrounding red

The Sedona area is too wet to be a desert, as shown by this Bear Wallow Canyon scene along Schnebly Hill Road. Lurking in the fog is the Mogollon Rim. Larry Lindahl

rocks and canyons. If you want to buy art, Sedona's 50-odd galleries now exhibit everything from reproductions of prehistoric pottery to incomprehensible abstract sculpture. If you just want to observe the interaction between modern *Homo sapiens* and a landscape that ought to humble us, but often doesn't, Sedona is the perfect stage set.

I still can't help mourning the Sedona that never was — a national park with 100 square miles of red hills and mountains and canyons with which nothing except Nature would ever get to tinker. My spine, which is stuffed with populist marrow, stiffens with the principle that a place of such profound beauty should be equally accessible — and equally inaccessible — to all. But my cortex blooms with hypocrisy. I ache with Red Rock Fever.

Dense vegetation lines Oak Creek near Midgely Bridge.
Larry Lindahl

When You Go

With an elevation of 4,500 feet, Sedona enjoys four distinct seasons, none too extreme. June, July, and August, however, routinely bring highs in the 90s. Midsummer nights, happily, sink to the 50s and 60s. Sedona entertains the most people during its mildest seasons: March through May and September through October. On weekends in these months, getting a room without a reservation may be impossible. Least crowded: the first two weeks of December and all of January.

Recommendation: Visit Sedona when the fewest people are visiting Sedona. Late fall and winter are lovely, and the occasional threat of rain, fog, or snow only enhances the experience — the red rocks become unpredictably different characters in the wet. The only disadvantages to a winter visit are the shorter days, which shrink the possibilities for outdoor activities, and the fact that some lodges in Oak Creek Canyon close for the season.

Sedona-area accommodations include forest campsites maintained by the Forest Service (see pages 50 and 59), private RV parks, motels, B&Bs, rustic cabins in Oak Creek Canyon, and world-class resorts. Timeshare condos are increasingly popular. For any of these, make reservations as far in advance as possible. The Sedona-Oak Creek Canyon Chamber of Commerce is very helpful; call (928) 282-7722 or (800) 288-7336 for assistance with lodging or a free information packet. Fax: (928) 204-1676.

If Sedona is full, stay in Cottonwood, 20 miles southwest on State Route 89A; or in Flagstaff, 30 miles north on State Route 89A. The Cottonwood-Verde Valley Chamber of Commerce phone number is (928) 634-7593. Flagstaff tourist information is (928) 774-9541 or (800) 842-7293. On the Web, visit www.flagstaff.arizona.org

The Internet is blooming with information on Sedona. A google.com search for the word "Sedona" turned up 164,000 Web sites containing everything from print-them-yourself Forest Service booklets to an omnium-gatherum of New Age mystica. Some of the more useful Web addresses are:

www.visitsedona.com (Sedona-Oak Creek Canyon Chamber of Commerce)

www.city.sedona.net (local resources)

www.redrocknews.com (Sedona Red Rock News, the city's twice-weekly newspaper)

A good way to get a sense of the community is to read the *Sedona Red Rock News* online, or subscribe to the quarterly *Sedona Magazine*, (928) 282-9022. Visitors from distant states or foreign countries generally fly into Phoenix Sky Harbor, the nearest major airport, and rent a car for the drive to Sedona, which takes about two hours. There is no regularly scheduled commercial passenger service to the Sedona Airport, which serves light aircraft with a 5,100-foot paved and lighted runway. (928) 282-4487.

The nearly universal mistake in visiting Sedona is squeezing the trip into too short a time. This is not chamber-of-commerce prattle; it's an observation from dozens of visits. Five to seven days is ideal. This allows one or two excursions to attractions such as the Grand Canyon, Jerome, the prehistoric ruins at Tuzigoot National Monument, or the Navajo Reservation (see Chapters 4 and 5), and enough time in the cradle of the red rocks to get a sense of the place.

Month	Average maximum (°F)	Average minimum (°F)	Average precipitation (inches)
January	55	30	1.70
February	59	32	1.54
March	63	35	1.67
April	72	42	1.17
May	81	49	0.56
June	91	57	0.49
July	95	65	1.89
August	92	64	2.42
September	88	58	1.51
October	78	49	1.16
November	65	37	1.32
December	56	31	1.79

CHAPTER TWO

Inside Sedona

The Arts Flourish

Top: Tlaquepaque re-creates an 18th-century Spanish Colonial village, with luminarias lighting the way at Christmas. Tom Bean Above: Richard Drayton's painting captures red rock country.

Opposite: Climate and landscape blend harmoniously with the music at Sedona's annual Jazz on the Rocks festival. Tom Johnson

All great art is the work of the whole living creature, body and soul, and chiefly of the soul.

— JOHN RUSKIN
19th-century English art critic

Not for the first time, Sedona artist Richard Drayton has painted the red rocks almost without using red paint. The craggy buttes on the canvas before us reveal a spectrum of possibly 50 shades of cream, peach, gold, orange, blue, magenta, purple, and indigo. But the only red is a tingling, luminescent hairline border on the rocks separating sunlight from shadow, and it's so subtle he has to point it out before I see it.

From this description, you'd expect Drayton's portraits of the Sedona landscape to be quirky and personal interpretations, but you'd be wrong. They are startlingly realistic. In fact, his redless paintings appear to capture more of the reality of the red rocks than the work of most painters.

Drayton smiles, absorbing pleasure in the compliment.

"It's taken me 10 years of painting the landscape to get to this point," he says.

Gallery owner Jim Ratliff

understands what Drayton discovered: "So many artists come here to paint the red rocks because they're enamored with the color, and they fail miserably. The paintings turn out flat. The reason is that they're missing the point. The red rocks aren't about color; they're about light."

True enough. But Sedona artists will tell you that their great rock garden is about much more. They will say it's about mystery, inspiration, obsession. About ineffable colors that glow in the mind even though they will not register on film or pixels. About the power this landscape has to transform an artist's vision, temperament, and way of seeing the world. And ultimately about the soul.

The Visual Arts

The red rocks have been luring artists to Sedona for more than half a century.

Max Ernst, the German surrealist, built a place here in 1950 and declared to his friends, "There are only two places in the world I want to live — Paris and Sedona." In 1961, the Egyptian-born sculptor Nassan Gobran and a few volunteers founded the Sedona Arts Center, which continues today as a nonprofit art school, gallery, and community theater. In 1965, Western artist Joe Beeler sat down at a table in the Oak Creek Tavern with three friends — Charlie Dye, John Hampton, and George Phippen — and formed the Cowboy

More than a million holiday lights create man-made splendor at Los Abrigados Resort.
Bob & Suzanne Clemenz

Artists of America. Before long there were an estimated 300 artists living and working in Sedona, and today more than 80 galleries are spanning a wide range of price, genre, and taste. One of them, Exposures International, founded by retired Los Angeles advertising executive Marty Herman, bills itself as Arizona's largest fine art gallery and exhibits work priced as high as $350,000.

Sedona no longer is just lovely landscapes and the romanticized West.

Long-time gallery owner Peggy Lanning-Eiseler said she has watched the art market mature, "though gradually, like a child growing up." Still, art that people might see as confrontational or baffling remains rare in Sedona. Bruce Tobias's The Select Art Gallery opened in 1995 and danced out on the cutting edge, up to and including live nude body painting. It closed four years later, with Tobias saying he wanted to devote more time to — what else? — his real estate business.

In *Scenic Sedona*, published by Arizona Highways in 1989, I observed that for all the diversity and quality of the art being created and sold in Sedona, none of it was combative or controversial, or even eccentric. Gallery owner Ratliff offered a theory that seemed intriguing and maybe right on target. There is an energy in the red rocks, he said; he didn't know what it is, but somehow it fuels the creative process.

"But it can only be used in a positive way," he said. "If people try to use that energy to create something negative, they don't stay around. The red rocks spit them right out of here."

Apparently that energy is still humming. There is more eccentric and sophisticated art around Sedona today, but no eruption of "negative" art. There is an influx of new people and new ideas, a growing national and international clientele, and with all that, an occasional controversy. Which is healthy.

Fuller Barnes, a talented and imaginative scrap-metal sculptor who moved to Sedona in 1992, fabricated a jagged dragon out of rusty car and tractor parts and parked it for a while in front of a real-estate office in town. People called, scolding the brokerage for displaying the image of Satan. The complaint was relayed to Barnes, who was ecstatic. "Well, great!" he exclaimed. "Now we know what he looks like."

What draws artists to Sedona? The answer seems obvious [just look around], but most of them are not here to paint the red rocks. The inspiration they draw from the place goes beyond red rocks.

D. Michael McCarthy cheerfully labels himself a throwback, a 19th-century Hudson River School painter time-warped into the modern world through some insidious trick of fate. His paintings contemplate romanticized, mystical mountains and heroic canyons of impossible proportions. His landscapes do not, could not, exist. But to anyone who knows Sedona, the pristine, iridescent light in them triggers the sense of déjà vu.

"Light really is the prime mover in my painting, and I've never lived anywhere else that had such a dramatic influence on my perception of it," he says.

"I'm interested in the larger workings of nature, the interactions of sky and earth, and this is where you can see it the most dramatically. The colors in this landscape are pretty harsh, and yet the light does wonderful things to them. For example, when rain is falling over the rim of a butte and there's a rainbow overhead, everything is muted. A lot of times I'll put an Arizona sky into a painting of someplace else."

Mike Medow is a sculptor and painter whose art focuses exclusively on the human form — females, to be precise, whose bodies are exaggerated and distorted for their fluidity of line,

not overt sexuality. He carves his sculptures in native alligator juniper, always a twisted, gnarled, unpredictable wood, working with chisels and rasps, never planning in advance but

Top: A bronze of Merlin by John M. Soderberg is juxtaposed with red rock country. Bob & Suzanne Clemenz Above: Artist D. Michael McCarthy's painting infuses Oak Creek Canyon with mystical qualities.

Below: Sedona sculptor Susan Kliewer's bronze of Sedona Schnebly stands in front of the Sedona Public Library. Bob & Suzanne Clemenz

allowing the wood to yield up the form that nature locked within it.

The light and landforms haven't affected his art, he says, but his introspective Sedona lifestyle has.

"There's not much for an adult to do here, after hiking," he says in an observation that will furrow brows over at the Chamber of Commerce, "so maybe it gives me more drive to stay busy. I'm forced to go deep within."

Sedona photographer Lou DeSerio makes his living portraying the surrounding landscape in the most literal way possible — big Cibachrome prints that render the extravagant colors and forms in minute detail. But it isn't just about surfaces for him, either.

"I like to think that this place produces a deeper look into oneself," he told me. "Sedona provides an environment where I can hear myself better, where I can connect, where I can evolve."

Sculptor Skip Fox landed in Sedona after a working life back East practicing dentistry. He and his wife, Elaine, a nutritionist, commissioned a house where on clear days they can see 90 miles in two compass directions and vividly colored mountain ramparts in the other two. Fox's sculpture has little to do with these landscapes but plenty to do with majesty and imagination.

"This vast vista expands minds," Fox said. "It opens things up. I don't know if you can see it in our work, but artists feel it."

The best news for the Sedona art buyer today is that the range of available work is wide and still expanding. The best news for the artists is that the community's

increased wealth and sophistication are feeding some of them very well. Fuller Barnes is making outdoor sculpture and furniture for Sedonans on commissions from $500 to $12,000. Usually his patrons trust his imagination.

"Mostly, the designs are left up to me," he said. "That's been terrific; I need that freedom."

But the worst news arrives in that same package of increased wealth and sophistication. The cost of housing in Sedona now flatly slams the door on struggling artists, and the rising rent on commercial space argues against galleries taking chances with art that might appeal only to a small, niche audience. Sedona artists and galleries can no longer afford failure, and that caution will shape their future.

One member of Sedona's performing arts community put it succinctly: "There's no market here for cutting-edge anything. People come here to get away from the cutting edge."

Architecture

If it were being proposed today, the Chapel of the Holy Cross could not be built. There would be furious controversy and a flurry of lawsuits. Someone such as Robert McConnell, once dean of the University of Arizona College of Architecture, would be called to testify.

"The best thing we architects can do for the mountains," he would say, "is to stay away from them."

Stars of the Milky Way rise into a moonlit sky over the Chapel of the Holy Cross. Frank Zullo

More than two decades ago, McConnell said precisely that to me in an interview, and I reflect on it every time I return to Sedona. Can a building ever enhance a mountain? Can architecture ever meld with nature so gracefully that it simply belongs?

Nearly always, a resounding No! But some of the Sinagua and Anasazi ruins of northern Arizona grow from their cliffside sites with such inevitability that they seem almost to invest the native rock with intelligence — as does the Chapel of the Holy Cross, Sedona's most inspired man-made landmark.

Marguerite Brunswig Staude, a Los Angeles sculptor born in 1899 to wealth and social prominence, had long been obsessed with the idea of a cathedral that would lead people to God through art —

contemporary art, not Gothic. In 1932, she attended a Lenten mass at St. Patrick's Cathedral in New York City and found herself thinking, as she later wrote, "How come the Church clings to its past glory while seeming totally to ignore the present, as though it did not exist?" She decided to commission her own cathedral. After World War II aborted a scheme for a Budapest site by

Tlaquepaque brings shopping to a Spanish Colonial setting.
Left: Tulips and a fountain define a courtyard. Bob & Suzanne Clemenz
Above: Shoppers inspect Native American creations. Tom Bean

Frank Lloyd Wright, she retained Anshen & Allen Architects of San Francisco, and together they selected this niche in the red rocks. Instead of a cathedral, it would be a small but dramatic chapel dedicated to the memory of her parents — "A spiritual fortress," she wrote, "so charged with God that it spurs man's spirit Godward!"

A more godly site would have been hard to find. The chapel, built in 1955-56, seems to thrust itself out of two rounded sandstone knobs. Twin Buttes thrusts vertically skyward behind it, like the stage set of some epic drama. The hillocks immediately around are gruff and angular and spiked with ocotillo and agave.

Anshen & Allen wisely decided not to try to upstage this natural spectacle, but they didn't hide their building in it, either. The architecture is simple to the point of austerity, which was much in vogue in the 1950s, but it is also confident and assertive. Imagine a concrete-aggregate cereal box with one narrow side removed so the long sides can splay outward, and a great concrete cross, 90 feet high, thrust through the center. This is all there is. No splash of color, no ornament, no articulation to break up those vast, flat walls. Inside, it is just as severe. No stained glass, no pipe organ. There are a handful of contemporary sculptures by Staude and others.

But it isn't a simple building. It exudes as many moods as the landscape around it. In the full sun, it has a defiant attitude.

"These rocks around may erode," it seems to say, "I will not."

But as the late afternoon sun fades and the rocks turn orange, then deep rust, the building retreats, absorbing the colors, going gently into the good night with the mountains. Then the full moon comes out and frosts the chapel in silver fire, and it seems like the last citadel of man standing alone in the universe.

I stayed outside watching the brittle moonlight finger the chapel one night, and I was transfixed. I thought back to a conversation with another dean of architecture, John Meunier of Arizona State University.

"If a building is worthy of contemplation, then it qualifies as architecture," Meunier said. "If it rewards that contemplation, then it's probably good architecture." This chapel rewards by enriching the human spirit. It is one of the rare buildings that justifies its intrusion in a glorious natural setting.

Tlaquepaque (pronounced "tlockay-pockay") likewise could not be built today. Half of it lies in Oak Creek's flood plain, and it crowds into an environmentally sensitive grove of 200-year-old Arizona sycamores.

But things were looser in 1971 when Nevada hotel and restaurant developer Abe Miller began building Tlaquepaque, named after an artists' colony in Guadalajara, Mexico, and modeled on an idealized 18th-century Spanish Colonial village. Miller originally planned to let artists live and work upstairs and sell their creations on the ground floor, but the Sedona art market of the '70s wasn't spinning off enough money to make that practical. Boutiques, galleries, and restaurants eventually occupied both levels of the village.

But Miller did not dilute the architecture of his dream. He loved Spanish Colonial Mexico and personally imported as much of it as he could to weave into Tlaquepaque: antique church doors, ornamental stone lintels, fountains, gates, bells, decorative wrought iron.

"He worked his tail off all his life," said his daughter, Marilyn Cordovano. "When he was finally in a position to be able to do Tlaquepaque, he was like a little kid in a candy store."

Miller also bowed to a historic treasure on the site: those hoary sycamores, their white trunks and branches poking and lurching in every direction. Any reasonable developer would have summoned the chain saws, first thing. But Miller envisioned the trees as an integral part of the architecture and braided the buildings around them. Branches writhe through passageways created especially for them, and verdant foliage embraces the arcades and towers. The trees tease the sunlight, breaking it up and making it benign. They harmonize so gracefully with the architecture that the whole development seems like one living organism.

Most of the modern attempts at Spanish Colonial revivalism in the Southwest are more like cartoons or clichés than real architecture. Tlaquepaque is unique in that it goes deeper and discovers the spirit of a different place and time, even though it

romanticizes the image. It exudes quiet dignity and provides intimate courtyards for relaxation or contemplation, qualities offered by few other shopping environments built in the late 20th century. Abe Miller, thankfully, was behind his time.

For a long time, Tlaquepaque and the chapel were the only buildings around town that took nothing away from the natural beauty around them. Lately, however, more and more private homes and public buildings are arising in harmony with — how else to say this? — the spirit of Sedona.

For example, drop into the Sedona Public Library, completed in 1995 by Design Group Architects, a small Sedona firm consisting of Mike Bower and Max Licher. Its form is based loosely on the historic apple-packing barns in Oak Creek Canyon, and its skin is a prehistoric Pueblo-like veneer of rough sandstone masonry, which automatically integrates the building into the colors and textures of the red rocks forming its backdrop. But like Drayton with his landscape paintings, Bower and Licher have spent enough time prowling the rocks to understand the great variations in their color — red, orange, pink, ocher, white, black. For the library, they actually ordered the stonemasons to use a prescribed percentage of each color of stone to build the walls.

"The more rock that we use," Licher says, "the more it could be a unifying element that would

give Sedona an architectural character of its own."

Enchantment Resort, designed by Phoenix architect George Christensen, is a praiseworthy lesson in humility. Its puebloesque casitas slip gracefully into the folds of Boynton Canyon northwest of town without any architectural fuss. And yet, when I hike in this favorite canyon, I can't help comparing it with the Sinagua cliff dwellings all around me: Without expert eyes, they can't be seen at all.

Performing Arts

Sedona Cultural Park, a 50-acre alfresco performing arts theater, opened in 2000 with a concert by the Phoenix Symphony Orchestra. Solo artists from BB King to Tony Bennett followed, along with the annual Jazz on the Rocks festival. The three monumental wooden arches soaring over the stage, up to 60 feet high and 125 feet at their bases, have crowned performances by everything from symphony orchestras to jazz, rock, pop, and country ensembles.

The arches symbolize Sedona's artistic aspirations. At this publication date, financial difficulties have caused the park to close; however, Sedonans, who worked for more than 20 years to create the park, seem determined to revive the quiescent venue.

The performing arts in

Right: Enchantment Resort fits without fanfare into Boynton Canyon, like a modern-day pueblo. Tom Johnson

Sedona are maturing quickly. It's a small city, so it must import much of its talent, but the audiences are hungry. The Canyon Moon Theater Company, founded in 1997, produces four light comedies or musicals each season, along with two or three more adventurous shows by playwrights such as Tom Stoppard. Shakespeare Sedona produces the Bard and other classics. And Chamber Music Sedona brings in a dozen classical ensembles annually.

Below: The Calder Quartet in performance. Photograph provided by Chamber Music Sedona.
Right: Jazz musician Norman Brown. Tom Johnson

But Jazz on the Rocks has been Sedona's prime performing arts attraction since 1982 when local pianist Johnny Gilbert put together the first alfresco show for a thousand jazz enthusiasts. By 1985 attendance had more than doubled, and planners decided they could shoot for the stars. Since then, the list of headliners at Jazz on the Rocks reads like a who's who of syncopation: the Count Basie Orchestra, Nancy Wilson, Dizzy Gillespie, Tuck and Patti, Big Bad Voodoo Daddy. Do the sapphire sky and red mountains inspire musicians as they do painters? Absolutely. Blues singer Doug MacLeod once recalled his first gig at Jazz on

the Rocks for *Arizona Highways*: "I remember standing on the stage, red rocks off to my left, red rocks off to my right. And a thought hit me: It's impossible to do a bad show in this place." A few years earlier, the festival booked the great drummer Louis Bellson and his wife, the legendary Pearl Bailey. She fell ill, but Bellson came anyway. He strolled the festival grounds, his eyes feasting, and said, "If Pearly was here, she would say, 'God lives here.'"

When You Go

Gallery cruising in Sedona can be exhilarating and exhausting. There are more than any reasonable human would want to visit in a week, and no published guide lists all the galleries with their current specialties. Fortunately, most of the galleries are sprinkled around town in three clusters: Along State Route 179 within a mile or so of the "Y" junction, in Tlaquepaque, and around uptown Sedona. Others are loosely scattered along State Route 89A in west Sedona. Art enthusiasts also will find day trips to Flagstaff and Jerome to be useful.

As more and more galleries open — In 2004 they numbered more than 80 — they increasingly specialize. Personal taste will suggest where you look. Specialties include Western, Southwestern/Native American, photography, landscape, whimsical contemporary, provocative contemporary, and New Age. Several galleries are eclectic and unpredictable.

Carry a notebook to help remind you where and what you saw that you liked. It is no breach of gallery etiquette to make a lower offer on a higher-priced piece, but it is unethical to try an end run by contacting the artist directly. Advice on buying prehistoric Indian artifacts: don't. Counterfeits and illegally obtained pieces abound. Contemporary pottery and legitimate reproductions are much better reminders of your northern Arizona experience.

The most important tip for anyone who wants to attend any of the festivals in Sedona is: Plan ahead, way ahead. Tickets sell out, rooms fill up. Six months ahead is not too early to book a room for Jazz on the Rocks.

The Sedona-Oak Creek Canyon Chamber of Commerce, (928) 282-7722 or (800) 288-7336, each year compiles a free calendar of events, which is a good place to start planning. It's available on the Web at: www.visitsedona.com. Here are some of the arts events and festivals:

March: Sedona International Film Festival. A weekend of workshops and screenings of independent, foreign, and documentary films. (928) 282-0747. Visit www.sedonafilmfestival.com.

May: Art and Sculpture Walk at the Radisson Poco Diablo Resort, sponsored by the Sedona Arts Center. (928) 282-3809.

July: Shakespeare Sedona. Evening and matinee performances throughout the month, with discussions following some. Visit www.shakespearesedona.com.

September: Jazz on the Rocks. Tickets go on sale June 1. The outdoor Saturday show may not sell out, but the intimate Friday night concert definitely will. Bring a blanket or a low-back beach chair to sit on. Hat and sunblock are musts for daylight performances. (928) 282-1985. Visit www.sedonajazz.com.

October: Sedona Arts Festival, a juried show with works of more than 125 artists from around the country. (928) 204-9456.

October-May: Chamber Music Sedona features diverse artists throughout the season. Concerts are held at St. John Vianney Church. (928) 204-2415. Visit www.chambermusicsedona.org.

Thanksgiving-January: Red Rock Fantasy of Lights at Los Abrigados. Sedona families deck the walls, trees, and lawns of the 22-acre resort with displays incorporating more than a million lights. (928) 282-1777.

The Chapel of the Holy Cross is open 9 A.M. to 5 P.M. daily. There is no Mass, but lay leaders from St. John Vianney Catholic Church conduct a public prayer service every Monday at 5 P.M. (928) 282-4069.

SEDONA IN SPIRIT

*Something deeply hidden
had to be behind things.*
— ALBERT EINSTEIN
*From a hand-written
autobiographical note*

No scenic attraction or environmental issue, ironically, has won Sedona as much international publicity — some of it, say the locals, unwanted — as the "vortexes." Is there some physical or metaphysical energy in the red rocks? How do these spiritual hot spots actually work? How does Sedona, with its soaring cost of living, keep attracting psychics and New Age entrepreneurs who haven't exactly lived a life of stock options?

Whatever one's feelings about geographical spirituality, it's significant here. A Northern Arizona University study in 1996 found that 64 percent of visitors were seeking some form of spiritual experience in Sedona. Of those, 43 percent specifically mentioned the vortexes.

The New Age arrived in Sedona in the early 1980s, as a few believers declared it one of the planet's "power points" — a place where an indefinable form of energy flowed freely out of the earth. Page Bryant, a self-proclaimed psychic, identified four concentrations, or "vortexes," of this energy within a few miles of town. Someone noted that the very name of the town appeared to be an electromagnetic omen: Sedona spelled backwards becomes Anodes, the plates in vacuum tubes that attract electrons.

In August, 1987, Sedona attracted 5,000 people — true believers and the merely curious — to the Harmonic Convergence, a planet-healing festival. At sunrise on Airport Mesa, one of the "vortexes," they formed circles of 12 people, chanted the Om mantra, raised their left arms to the sky and pointed their right arms downward to direct positive energy into the earth. Some directed their aspirations toward the stars, buying $150 tickets to sit on Bell Rock at the moment it was supposed to depart for the galaxy of Andromeda. Which it failed to do.

But as Warren Cremer, a cultural anthropologist who ran a Jeep tour business, told me shortly afterward, "That was the exception. The movement has a clean intent. I don't see cranks or cults; I see people who are no longer satisfied with establishment medicine, science, or religion, and are looking for something else. They don't know how to go about it, exactly, but they're definitely non-confrontational, non-protestational. They're looking for a better planet and a better way of life, and in that, I support the community 100 percent."

Cremer's moderate line wasn't taken by all. Some who came after the Harmonic Convergence claimed to have experiences that can only be filed under woo-woo.

In a book titled *Sedona Starseed*, author Raymond Mardyks claimed, "There exists deep within Boynton Canyon an area used as a teleportation instrument . . . the Beings who travel (these) holes in space are from a planet that orbits an invisible star near Sirius."

In *Sedona: Psychic Energy Vortexes*, Dick Sutphen reported that a visitor laid some crystals beside a dry creek bed and watched a giant Indian woman rise from the canyon floor: "She stood about 200 feet tall and was dressed in white buckskin . . . she was beautiful."

New Agers also began building medicine wheels — circles of rocks five to 200 feet in diameter — on Coconino National Forest land around Sedona. Disciples called them a "reawakening of Native American wisdom." The Forest Service called them pollution.

But increasingly, Sedona's New Age community is merging into the mainstream. "As a group, we're being seen more as an integral part of the community," said Craig Junjulas, a teacher of workshops on self-discovery. "We're being taken more seriously." Junjulas heads a group of business people calling themselves the Sedona Metaphysical Spiritual Association, and they are bona fide members of the Chamber of Commerce. Every April they sponsor an Earth Day celebration, staging medicine wheel celebrations and classes such as "Seeing the Human Aura" and "Working with Healing Energy."

Junjulas explained how he disarms the occasional detractor. "Please don't call me 'space cadet'," he'll say. "I've been doing this for 20 years,

Bell Rock: $150 for a seat
and still it failed to depart for
Andromeda. George Stocking

so it's 'captain' or 'admiral.' When you approach them with humor, it breaks down their defenses."

Pete A. Sanders Jr. also conducts spiritual workshops. In an afternoon's conversation, he proved to be a reasonable spokesman for the vortex phenomenon, as convincing as anyone could be across the table from a skeptic. Sanders said he has a degree in biomedical chemistry from the Massachusetts Institute of Technology and skipped

out on Harvard Medical School to pursue unconventional research into human mental, physical, and spiritual potential. This brought him to Sedona.

Sanders said the vortexes around Sedona come in two forms: upflow, where energy bursts out of the earth; and inflow, where it goes in. Sometimes these are cataloged as male and female vortexes. Upflow/male vortexes are mountain or mesa tops; inflow/female vortexes are associated with depressions and canyons. Male vortexes are energizing; females encourage introspection.

New Agers consider Cathedral Rock
to be a feminine vortex. Larry Lindahl.

"If you go to these sites," Sanders said, "you literally see people walking differently. At some, they're chin down and reflective. At others, tall and confident. I'm hypothesizing that the same way there are currents in oceans and in the atmosphere, there are extradimensional currents in these sites that orient people's perceptions, and that we can 'ride' these currents in the same way that hawks and eagles ride thermals."

Both kinds of vortexes are valuable, he said. People come to Sedona trying to work things out, seeking inspiration "to be the best we can be, whether that comes through faith in God or faith in perseverance." The energy flow helps get us out of "our little bitty selves."

Despite his background, Sanders couldn't call his metaphorical hawks and eagles to earth. He doesn't know what kind of energy keeps them soaring or searching. He can't say whether belief in it is a matter of science, philosophy, or religion.

"It shouldn't be an either/or," he said. "Science is not the end-all of what is. It's just what we know so far."

I remain a vortex agnostic. I have been to all of the sites and have had no spiritual epiphanies, no tinglings of insight or energy. But I did once find myself on a Jeep tour of vortex sites with a clinical psychologist, a smart woman who was not predisposed to believe, either.

At the last stop, our guide nodded to one side, and said, "The energy comes from over there."

"No," the psychologist said, looking in a different direction. "It's coming from over there."

When You Go

All the Sedona vortexes, or power points, are easy to find. They tend to be busy. If lonely meditation is what you're seeking, go at dawn.

Bell Rock is the bell-shaped monolith off State Route 179 5.5 miles south of its "Y" junction with State Route 89A. There is no official trail and no agreed-upon point to experience the vortex power. Hikers and energy seekers have marked numerous routes to the upper mezzanines. The summit is difficult and intimidating; only spiders and rock climbers go there. This is said to be a masculine vortex.

Cathedral Rock is a feminine vortex, a ridge stretched between two peaks that offers awesome views. For directions, see Page 52.

Airport Mesa demands little or no hiking. Drive 1.1 miles on State 89A west of the "Y" junction and turn south on Airport Road. Some sources recommend parking at the dirt pullout half a mile up the mesa and walking east up the short trail. Others suggest driving all the way to the top and following the signs to the "Sunrise Service" and the Masonic Lodge Memorial Cross. This is a masculine vortex.

Boynton Canyon exudes both masculine and feminine energy, believers say. For directions, see Page 52. Some people climb up to formations in the canyon walls that seem to have energy or personal meaning to them. One hoodoo, or strangely shaped formation, on the east wall offers a womb-like space.

CHAPTER THREE

Outside Sedona

Amid Arizona's Finest

Sedona's climate and terrain invite people to get active.
Top: Jeeps take visitors right into the heart of red rock country, with Munds Mountain in the background. Tom Bean
Above: This bike rider extracts excitement from the red rocks in the Cow Pies area. Mike Padian
Right: The reward for pedaling up Schnebly Hill Road can be solitude and a fantastic view. Mike Padian

I am alarmed when it happens that
I have walked a mile
into the woods bodily, without
getting there in spirit . . .
what business have I in the woods,
if I am thinking
of something out of the woods?
— HENRY DAVID THOREAU
from his essay, Walking

Great, fat drops of rain begin to splatter the windshield just 30 seconds after I've paid my eight bucks for admission to Slide Rock State Park 7 miles north of Sedona. I expected it—a sky the color of a stealth bomber's belly usually will do something like this.

But the rain doesn't ruin the day, not here. I wrap myself in a rain jacket and Seattle sombrero and leave the car for a day of hiking in Oak Creek Canyon and its tributaries. I stare at the towering west wall of the canyon, and even in the softness of the rain, the red and charcoal palisade assumes the craggy, Olympian mood of a late Beethoven sonata. Its power and mystery seem palpable. Low clouds probe into side canyons like ghosts slinking through dark alleys. Rain, splashing onto the sandstone sluice framing Oak Creek, paints it the color of a

glistening king salmon fillet. Its improbable brilliance recalls the story about a Wisconsin pressman who, decades ago, throttled back the color on an *Arizona Highways* press run because he refused to believe rocks existed in such outrageous shades of red.

No rain check — who needs one? I'd pay double to be out here in this weather. The crowds evaporate. The creek begins to thrash more urgently. The natural drama of the canyon is enhanced. There is more than ever to see, a constellation of fresh extravaganza in the landscape. Thoreau, were he around, would find his thoughts fully engaged in the landscape at hand because it is so lovely and dramatic. I rarely daydream in the woods around Sedona. There's just not enough leftover brain capacity for it.

This is the best place to be outdoors in Arizona. The climate is amenable to all-season hiking, with a range of elevation from 4,000 feet around Red Rock Crossing to 7,122 feet atop Wilson Mountain. The variety of scenery is astonishing and the supply of surprises inexhaustible. An unheralded Sinagua pueblo suddenly pops into view on the Lost Canyon Trail. A bizarre copse of oak trees, their trunks all curling in unison to the south, greets me at Sterling Pass. There are wonderful sights to be bagged with hardly any exertion. Seven Sacred Pools, a queue of rain-collecting dimples on a sandstone ledge, is a half-mile stroll from the end of Soldier Pass Road.

And then there are routes that feel, with a full pack, more like death marches than hikes.

This lovely land can be hazardous as well, another characteristic that recommends Thoreauvian attention to the matters at hand. Rattlesnakes, for one. No need to fear, just be aware — and learn from the occasional encounters. I once met a diamondback on a trail in Sycamore Canyon 20 miles south of Sedona. We made eye contact from a respectful distance and engaged in a wordless negotiation: I agreed to circle 10 feet out of my way and not disturb his sunbath, and he agreed to not terminate my existence. I reflected on this episode during the next hour. Negotiations with Nature are always clear and unambiguous. She never lies, never complains, never explains. We invite trouble

This 90-foot-long natural bridge is Fay Arch, one of the landmarks in the Red Rock-Secret Mountain Wilderness.
Bob & Suzanne Clemenz

shouldn't do that."

There are several other guidelines for any form of outdoor recreation in the Sedona area. In addition to the standard caveats that apply to hiking and camping anywhere, remember these:

• Always carry more water than you think you'll need. The dry air, mountain topography, and steep rise in daytime temperature can cause dehydration sooner than you might expect. The standard formula for desert or arid mountain hiking applies everywhere around Sedona: one gallon per person per day.

• High elevation and bright sunlight mean a high risk of sunburn and, more ominously, melanoma. Wear a hat and use sunblock. Yes, in winter, too.

• That same high elevation and clear atmosphere translates into a serious risk of hypothermia if you're surprised by a storm or lost after dark. Temperatures plunge. Carry extra clothing, emergency food, a flashlight, and waterproof matches.

• Wear hiking boots. Most of the trails around the red rocks involve some steep ascending or slickrock scrambling where good traction is vital. And don't commit fully to a foothold or handhold until you're certain you can trust it. Sandstone can crumble like a stale scone.

• Most Coconino National Forest trails in the area are

only when we show up without adequate respect.

Years ago, when I began hiking in the Sedona area, I lurched to the summit of Wilson Mountain. Alone and exhausted, I took out a Forest Service leaflet and read that the mountain was named for Richard Wilson, who had been grim-reaped right here in 1885, by a bear. I quietly slinked 3,000 feet back down to civilization and called Bob Gillies, then the ranger in charge of the Forest Service office in Sedona. He said he had not heard of any bear incidents in modern history. Sure, there are bears, he's seen them, but they stay away from people. Except: "If you have one cornered . . . " he began, then paused, hunting for the right words. ". . . Well, you just

• Fishing is allowed anywhere on public property bordering Oak Creek with a state license. Arizona Game and Fish stocks it with non-native rainbow trout all year, most frequently in summer.

• Jeep tours have long been a popular and painless way to visit the back country around Sedona. Specialized tours target archaeological sites, vortexes, or photo opportunities. You can also rent a jeep locally and drive it yourself.

• Aircraft tours provide another perspective. At this writing, adventurers can choose from hot-air balloons, helicopters, and open-cockpit biplanes.

• Weddings among the red rocks are a booming cottage industry. Several local planners

Left: Trout lurk in the rocky underside of Oak Creek. Below: A Jeep scrambles just off Schnebly Hill Road. Both by Bob & Suzanne Clemenz Right: Fat-tired bikes were made for terrain like this area called Cow Pies. Mike Padian

multi-use, so follow this trail etiquette: mountain bikes yield to hikers and horses; hikers yield to horses.

• If you're parking anywhere in the National Forest, you'll need a "Red Rock Pass" ($5/day, $20 or $40 annually; the $20 pass excludes four particularly popular sites). The passes are available at various visitor centers in town and some trailheads.

Rainbow Trout And Lifetime Vows

Since Sedona's tourism boom began, people have been discovering and inventing opportunities to experience the landscape. Some of this you can do on your own; in other cases, local for-profit enterprises are set up to guide you.

• Swimming is possible in tiny Oak Creek, most rewardingly at Grasshopper Point (just off State Route 89A between Mileposts 376 and 377) and at Slide Rock State Park.

arrange settings, music, photography, catering, and honeymoons.

Golf

Four courses are open to the public: Radisson Poco Diablo Resort and Canyon Mesa Country Club have nine-hole courses, and Sedona Golf Resort and Oak Creek Country Club offer 18 holes. Scenery is everywhere a hazard to concentration.

Mountain Biking

Red rock topography is steep and bumpy, but no need to be discouraged — modern mountain bikes employ front and rear suspensions to buffer the pain before it reaches the rider's rump. Local bike shop owner Rama Jon said the average age of resident mountain bikers in Sedona is probably 10 years older than anywhere else in the Southwest; one local club calls itself "The Gnarly Old Dudes."

The attractions of biking in the region include an increasingly well-marked trail system that's easily accessible from town — "Pick any compass direction from this shop and we can be on the dirt in 15 or 20 minutes," said Jon. Another surprise: no antagonism on the trails. "The hikers talk to the bikers; the bikers talk to the horses. Everybody gets along."

Jon's favorite biking: the Secret Trail system starting at the Midgley Bridge in Oak

These campers have set up on Steamboat Rock in the Red Rock-Secret Mountain Wilderness. Tom Bean

Creek Canyon, the Cockscomb in west Sedona, and Broken Arrow off Morgan Road. And for those not enchanted by dirt, there's the new wide-shouldered, four-lane State Route 89A connecting Sedona and Cottonwood — a smooth 20-mile ride flanked grandly by scenic mountains and desert.

Rock Climbing

Why go climbing in the red rocks?

"Because they're close," said Dave Keeber, Sedona Library director and climbing enthusiast. "And because rock climbers are nuts."

Seriously, although rock climbing is growing in popularity here, Sedona is no place for the inexpert climber. The formations are tantalizing, but the material is treacherous. The Kaibab (red) and Coconino (tan) sandstone of the red rocks is very soft and crumbly.

Keeber recommends one basalt cliff, which is much more stable: directly under Oak Creek Vista where State 89A climbs out of Oak Creek Canyon.

Camping

In 1995, the Forest Service estimated that 200,000 people camped somewhere in the woods, mountains, and canyons around Sedona. That number rang alarms in the service's rustic office on Brewer Road, because the number was more than foresters believed the environment could bear. Public land around Sedona now is officially closed to car and RV camping, except in developed campgrounds. Backpack camping is still allowed in the

Red Rock-Secret Mountain and Munds Mountain wilderness areas, but hikers must hoof at least a mile from any trailhead before pitching a tent.

Forest Service campgrounds in Oak Creek Canyon offer about 170 spaces. Most are first-come, but Pine Flat and Cave Springs have some reservable slots.

MANZANITA (between mileposts 380 and 381). Water, toilets, RVs up to 22 feet, no trailers. Open year around. 18 sites.

BOOTLEGGER (milepost 383). Toilets available, tent camping only. Open April 15 through Oct. 31. 10 sites.

CAVE SPRINGS (milepost 385.8). Water, toilets, showers. RVs and trailers to 36 feet, open April 15 through Oct. 15. 82 sites.

PINEFLAT EAST/PINEFLAT WEST (milepost 386.5). Water, toilets, RVs and trailers to 36 feet. West campground open March 1, east April 1; both through Nov. 15. 58 sites, including two handicap-accessible.

Hiking

Sedona is surrounded by the Coconino National Forest with two designated wilderness areas — the Red Rock-Secret Mountain to the north and the Munds Mountain to the south. Between them, and on adjoining state-owned lands, are more than 100 hikes. Some follow well-maintained and signed Forest Service trails, some take advantage of four-wheel drive or horse trails, and still others are informal routes catalogued by assorted private guidebooks. All

these vary greatly in accessibility and difficulty, but they have one thing in common: None is dull.

But some are crowded. Trails such as Boynton Canyon and the West Fork of Oak Creek can resemble lemming-runs on high-season weekends, putting reflective quiet in short supply. For best results, save these trails for a rainy day [literally] or hit them early on a midweek morning. The less-known and tougher trails are inviting any time.

Consider the season when planning a hike. Shady forest trails above 6,000 feet may be blocked by snow or ice in winter. Exposed desert routes are less enchanting in summer, although half-day hikes from dawn to late morning are cool enough in Sedona even in July. Here are 10 glorious and geatly varied day hikes in the Sedona area. The first eight weave around and upon the red rocks, and the last two start in Oak Creek Canyon. Mileages are one way, and difficulty ratings assume an experienced, middle-aged hiker of average ability and determination — me. Remember that a Red Rock Pass is required at all these except Baldwin Trail and the West Fork of Oak Creek, which assess a separate $5 per car parking fee.

LITTLE HORSE TRAIL (1.5 miles, easy) is an exquisite introduction to the majesty of the red rocks, since it skirts the bases of several of the monoliths. It also used to be an invitation to get lost among

Cathedral Rock Trail climbs 760 feet in less than a mile. David H. Smith

them thanks to the many false trails meandering off, but the Forest Service has improved it with better marking, a new trailhead with parking and toilet, and an information kiosk. Look for the trailhead on State Route 179 between Mileposts 309 and 310.

CATHEDRAL ROCK TRAIL (0.7 mile, moderate) is short but very steep, climbing 760 feet in less than a mile. The Forest Service has marked it with permanent wire-basket cairns and has chiseled helpful footholds in the sandstone. Trail's end is a crescent-shaped saddle between the sheer vertical towers of the "cathedral," with great views of the riparian scribble of Oak Creek. This is a "feminine" vortex, said to be good for unwinding from a high-stress job. Go 3.4 miles south on State Route 179 from the Sedona "Y", turn right on "Back-o-Beyond," and drive 0.7 mile to trailhead parking.

BALDWIN TRAIL (0.5 mile, easy) meanders through the dense and lovely riparian forest along Oak Creek from gloriously photogenic Red Rock Crossing to Cathedral Rock, then connects to the Templeton and Cathedral Rock trails. Drawbacks are a fee to park at the Forest Service's Red Rock Crossing-Crescent Moon site and a bit of boulder-hopping to cross the creek. Take Upper Red Rock Loop Road 2 miles to Chavez Ranch Road and follow the signs to the Red Rock Crossing-Crescent Moon day-use site.

BELL ROCK PATHWAY (3 miles, easy) is also a bike trail that parallels State 179. Vortex

seekers can take the 0.75-mile spur loop to a shelf up on the bell (but not all the way to the pointy summit). The north end of the trail adjoins the Little Horse trailhead; the south is at Milepost 312.1.

BOYNTON CANYON TRAIL (3 miles, easy) is, with good reason, the Sedona area's most popular hike; the red canyon walls contain and define a miniature world of drop-dead geological and botanical beauty. You'll hike through a forest of manzanita and visit (in season) the rapids of a foot-wide creek. There are perhaps 50 Sinagua ruins in this canyon, all so well concealed by their prehistoric architects you'll probably never see them. The Forest Service has banned hiking to the ruins because of Native American concerns. Take Dry Creek Road 2.9 miles north from State Route 89A in west Sedona, turn left on Boynton Pass Road and drive 1.6 miles to trailhead parking.

FAY CANYON TRAIL (1.1 miles, easy to moderate) offers the option of a scramble up a steep, unmaintained trail for a firsthand encounter with a natural arch. Take the fork to the right at the half-mile mark if you're up for the adventure; otherwise you won't see the arch from the main trail. Take Dry Creek Road 2.9 miles north from State 89A in west Sedona. Turn left on Boynton Pass Road. Look for trailhead parking on the right a half mile after the road turns to gravel.

HUCKABY TRAIL (2.6 miles,

Hikers climb a trail above Wet Beaver Creek. Tom Bean

Previous spread: This hiker stands atop Soldier Pass as he scans Lost Canyon. Larry Lindahl
Left: From atop Devils Arch, a hiker sees for miles into the Red Rock-Secret Mountain Wilderness, but west Sedona is only a few miles behind him. Laurence Parent
Right: A half-mile stroll brings you to Seven Sacred Pools, which are rain-collecting natural depressions in the rock. Coffee Pot Rock is in the background. Larry Lindahl

moderate), new in 1998, offers a panoply of terrain and views, from ridgetop overlooks of Sedona to the riparian woods astride Oak Creek. A boulder-hop is required; take care if the creek is running high. Take State Route 179 for 0.3 mile south from the Sedona "Y" and turn left on Schnebly Hill Road. Follow Schnebly Hill Road 0.8 mile to the turnoff signed for the Huckaby trailhead.

SOLDIER PASS TRAIL (0.5 mile, easy) is really just a stroll to a string of rain-collecting natural scoops in a cascade of sandstone ledges. They're known locally as the "Seven Sacred Pools." It's definitely worth investigation if there's been rain in the last few days. Take Soldier Pass Road 1.5 miles north from State Route 89A in west Sedona, turn right and park at the end of the last subdivision.

STERLING PASS TRAIL (2.4 miles, strenuous) corkscrews 1,120 feet up the west wall of Oak Creek Canyon to a weird copse of oak trees, all straining southward to grasp the spare light. Although the trail is heavily wooded, there are several spectacular viewpoints into the canyons below along the way. Take State 89A into Oak Creek Canyon; trailhead is 0.6 mile north of Milepost 380. There is little dedicated parking; do your best.

WEST FORK OF OAK CREEK (3 miles, moderate) should be renamed The Canyon the Moon Cannot Find, the irresistible and evocative title given it by the late *Arizona Highways* writer William E. Hafford. This is one of Arizona's great hikes, a cool, shadowy canyon where concave walls leap over the creek like ocean waves frozen for eternity. The first 3 miles are relatively flat and easy, although wading is seasonally necessary. Experienced backpackers can continue, with some difficulty, nine more miles. Take State 89A 10 miles north of Sedona. Fee parking is just north of Milepost 384.

Finally, for visitors who want a sampler of red rock hiking without the word "wilderness" hanging around, Red Rock State Park offers a 5-mile network of easy trails. Rangers or volunteers give guided nature walks daily at 10 A.M., and there are guided full-moon hikes twice each month, April through October (call for dates and times).

Left: The going's relatively easy for the first 3 miles of the trail along the West Fork of Oak Creek. Then, as this hiker sees, the canyon narrows, and hiking turns to rock scrambling. Tom Bean
Above: Rain produces ephemeral waterfalls in Oak Creek Canyon. Robert G. McDonald

When You Go

For further hiking and camping information, contact Coconino National Forest, Red Rock Ranger District, P.O. Box 300, Sedona, AZ 86339. (928) 282-4119. Fax: (928) 203-7539. For reservations at Pine Flats and Cave Springs campgrounds, call the Forest Service's national reservation service, (877) 444-6777.

Red Rock State Park is at 4050 Lower Red Rock Loop Road, Sedona, AZ 86336. (928) 282-6907.

Slide Rock State Park is just north of Milepost 381 on State Route 89A in Oak Creek Canyon. (928) 282-3034. The park charges an admission fee. Call for current price schedule.

For information on guided tours and recreational equipment rentals, contact the Sedona-Oak Creek Canyon Chamber of Commerce, P.O. Box 478, Sedona, AZ 86339. (928) 282-7722 or (800) 288-7336.

Photographing Sedona:
THE PROMISED LAND

To a photographer arriving from almost anywhere else, Arizona looks like the promised land. The bravura landforms, the drama of fierce light and cryptic shadow, the choreography of gunmetal thunderclouds rumbling over a mountain or canyon offer endless opportunities — and challenges. Photographing Arizona can be a life's work.

In fact, photographing a 20-mile radius around Sedona could be a life's work. The intrigue and beauty are extravagant, and the weather guarantees eternal variety. Sedona is not only a place artists move to; it's a place where people become artists.

Sedona doesn't ask for much specialized equipment, but a tripod is very helpful. You'll be shooting low-light pictures at dawn or dusk. If you're using a film camera, an 81a filter will subtly warm up dark skies and deep shadows. If you're shooting digital, you can reduce the bluish tint in computer editing. With film, a polarizing filter will darken a sun-bleached sky; with digital, you can intensify the contrast later. But don't go too far; the Red Rocks are no cartoon.

Sedona does ask for patience. As far as photography is concerned, the red rocks pale in the conditions we humans like best: warm, dry air and clear, blue sky. You can use this time for

So don't go there on a typical evening. Save such obvious shots for lousy weather, when everyone else will be indoors cursing the rain, and you'll have a chance of engaging the landscape in a different mood. Oak Creek Canyon's fall color party can be just another pretty photographic cliché, so search for the telling detail. A single golden sycamore leaf floating in a pool probably will tell a more powerful story than blotches of color on a distant mountainside.

When I photograph Sedona, I'm armed with ideas I've absorbed from working with dozens of photographers who spend a major part of their lives putting Arizona on film. Here are three excellent tips:

• The "180-degree rule" from Gary Ladd: When shooting landscapes in any dramatic lighting, turn around frequently to see what's happening behind you.

• The "near-far" technique of David Muench: Build a landscape from the nearest detail to the farthest horizon with every element in focus. This not only makes a sharp artistic statement, but an affirmation that all nature is a community, each piece equally vital to the integrity of the whole.

• "Creative patience" from Sedona's Bob Clemenz: "A lot of people get overwhelmed by the place and start shooting wildly. One of the things we do [in annual Sedona photographic workshops] is make four-by-five-inch cardboard 'picture finders.' Then we have the students put their cameras down. Somehow, they get a lot more creative with the finders. But probably the best advice for any photographer here is simply to stay around for a few days and begin to know the place."

Good advice, indeed. The only trouble is that it may turn a weekend affair into a lifetime obsession.

scouting locations and planning angles for sunset and sunrise shots. The rocks will appear the deepest red at sunset, because any dust in the air kicked up by the day's breeze will color the late light in the amber-orange-red end of the spectrum. But you won't have much time; sunsets in dry, clear air spoil quickly. I once measured the window of opportunity for an evening session with Cathedral Rock: seven minutes. Any shots earlier or later would have been wasting film.

Finding fresh images of Sedona may seem like a daunting challenge. Red Rock Crossing is sometimes said to be the most photographed scene in Arizona, which is easy to believe on a typical evening — a dozen photographers will be out there hopping rocks in the creek, jockeying for position.

CHAPTER FOUR

Day Trips

Ventures to Oak Creek Canyon,
Ancient Sites, the Verde Valley, and Jerome

Residents of Verde Valley and nearby mountains have left different imprints of their culture. Top: The Sinagua people left stories with figures carved into rocks. Larry Lindahl Above: A mansion in Jerome built by copper-mining magnate James

Douglas remains as Jerome State Historic Park and a symbol of the wealth extracted from the mountains. George H.H. Huey Right: Copper is a color in this legacy left by nature in Oak Creek Canyon. Bob & Suzanne Clemenz

The very forest-fringed earth seemed to have opened into a deep abyss, ribbed by red rock walls and choked by steep mats of green timber. The chasm was a V-shaped split and so deep that looking downward sent at once a chill and a shudder over Carley . . . What a wild, lonely, terrible place!

— ZANE GREY
from The Call of the Canyon *(1924)*

Night fell on a Sinagua Indian ruin under the brow of a red sandstone butte some 20 miles from midtown Sedona. In the last moments of light, the surrounding mountains seemed to turn violet, then smoky purple, then black against an indigo sky. There was a visitor here, a wilderness guide who went by the name of Ropes. He sensed that something was wrong.

"I'd been coming to this ruin in the daylight for 15 years," he said. "Once it got dark, it seemed so different. I got a real uneasy feeling — like I was intruding."

Ropes was no flake. He seemed to know as much about the ruin as an archaeologist. He knew that night, for example,

that he was bunking down in what might have been a nursery. The winter sun would have angled in to make this the warmest room in the pueblo, and there were impressions of tiny fingerprints that had been pressed into the red clay mortar in the walls 800 years ago. He also suspected that beneath the bare earth floor were burial sites. A Sinagua custom was to bury children's bodies under the pueblo, possibly so their spirits would benefit from the proximity of living parents.

"I was on the verge of drifting off to sleep," Ropes told me. "And then I heard crying. At first, I tried to tell myself that it was bats. Then I thought, well, it's jackrabbits. Finally I realized I was hearing children. Crying, in this room. I kind of chilled out, let the hair come back down on my neck, tried to go to sleep again. And every time I was on the verge of sleep, I'd be awakened by these ungodly sounds. Children crying. It felt like tears in there. All night, it felt like tears."

Ropes' experience may have been unnatural, but it isn't unusual. Wherever Southwestern prehistory is exposed, as it is all around Sedona, you hear variations on it. People encounter crows or snakes around the ruins and have the disquieting feeling that they aren't ordinary animals, but sentinels. Or they find a "souvenir" artifact, take it home, and suffer an inexplicable string of illnesses and accidents. Several years ago, after I had collected a substantial file of these stories, I phoned three archaeologists for comment. I

expected them to scoff. They didn't. Two of the three described strange encounters they had had.

Of course, there are many attractions other than prehistoric pueblos in northern Arizona, and most of us have perfectly normal and pleasant experiences when we do visit the ruins — in the daylight. But the land itself is enchanted; it frequently works magic on our spirits and emotions.

"Certain places take us beyond ourselves," wrote Flagstaff author Scott Thybony in *Burntwater*, and such places seem to present themselves in whatever direction a traveler radiates from Sedona.

Most visitors never investigate the wealth of possibilities within a two- or three-hour drive, and their lives — I think — are poorer for the failure. I've been having breakfast with assorted strangers at a Sedona bed-and-breakfast, and someone will say, "We have a whole day. What should we see?" I stifle the urge to scold — a week should be mandatory — and fetch an Arizona map.

Oak Creek Canyon

Zane Grey's 1924 novel *The Call of the Canyon* could have profited if he had shed a few adjectives from the overheated prose, or so I thought before I talked with Bob Kittredge. Wild, lonely, terrible? Oak Creek Canyon had never seemed so to me, not with 2.9 million cars a year beetling along the 12 miles of State Route 89A on the canyon floor. But Kittredge had grown up in the canyon in the

1950s, in a log cabin by the creek, and his childhood memories reflected Grey's descriptions.

It was indeed lonely, he said. Civilization seemed as distant as another planet. His company was not the birds and chipmunks that charm

tourists today, but an old radio he kept by the bed, pulling in clear channel KOMA from some place called Oklahoma City. A family excursion to Phoenix was a major production; the drive each way then took four or five hours.

There was one advantage, he said: "I learned very early to be resilient. I had to depend on myself for my entertainment."

But to a little kid, the canyon was overpowering. The scale of everything was too large. Once the sight of a bear cub, a plump fur ball hardly larger than a dog, scared him out of his wits. At

Oak Creek usually runs clear, cold, and shallow, coursing its way over rocks and under a canopy of tree limbs. Dick Dietrich

night, the trees were shadowy monsters with arms poised to snatch him. Once he fell off a horse while crossing Oak Creek, and it seemed like a river 60 feet wide.

He grew up and moved away.

"I swore I would never come back here," he told me. When he tentatively returned many years later, he felt claustrophobic. There were no horizons, only canyon walls squeezing away the sky.

"I finally came to feel the canyon as a place of refuge," he said, "but it's been a long process. And I find it interesting that none of the kids who grew up here at the time I did today lives in the canyon — or, for that matter, in any canyon."

Drive the highway, stop briefly at the popular attractions, and you are unlikely to feel such complicated sensations. But Oak Creek Canyon is still an easy place to get lost, figuratively, and when you are alone with the canyon, it can be a very powerful place.

The first English-speaking human to stake a claim to the canyon was Jim Thompson, an Irishman who ran away from home in Londonderry at 11, then kicked around the Wild West as a pioneering jack-of-all-trades. When he found his way into Oak Creek Canyon in 1876 at what is now called Indian Gardens (Milepost 378), he found, literally, Indian gardens of corn, squash, and beans. The Tonto Apaches had farmed the site not long before, and some of their crops were still popping up. Thompson built a log cabin, began cultivating his own crops, and eventually brought his family.

A trickle of pioneers followed. In 1907, Frank Pendley homesteaded a sloping meadow above Slide Rock, trapped bobcats for bounty, and planted fruit trees. His orchards, now on state park land, still produce apples. In 1930, Kittredge's father, Bob Sr., bought property and a dream and, 16 years later, moved out

With the San Francisco Peaks on the horizon, Oak Creek Canyon unfolds to the north from Mount Wilson.
Larry Lindahl

from New York because he craved solitude. Soon a sprinkling of rustic tourist cabins appeared. By the 1950s, the fact that Oak Creek Canyon had that one vital amenity, a paved road through it, guaranteed, for better or worse, that it would become one of Arizona's most popular destinations.

The first thing you notice, funneling into the canyon from Sedona, are the tops of the canyon walls. They aren't planar ridgelines butting against the sky, but an arcade of fanciful sculptures: a mitten, a thumb, a potbellied gargoyle. Layers of sandstone and limestone, each of a different texture and strength, have eroded and crumbled into cartoons.

The creek itself is another lovely attraction, a cold, crystalline, all-season waterway in a state where nearly every other river runs unreliably or ruddy with sediment. Unless it's

been raining heavily somewhere in its watershed, Oak Creek runs just two or three feet deep and 10 to 15 feet wide, gurgling a desultory course around smooth, black boulders, shaded by oak and sycamore trees that in many places form a full canopy across the water. Fish (and therefore fishermen) find it an amenable habitat — more than 20 species live in the creek, and the Arizona Game and Fish Department stocks it with non-native rainbow trout.

Slide Rock State Park, the old Pendley homestead, is the

Above: Garland's Oak Creek Lodge is tucked neatly alongside Oak Creek, providing civilized pleasures. Bob & Suzanne Clemenz
Left: Slide Rock State Park is a place where crowds frolic in the water and slide down a natural sandstone sluice. Dick Dietrich

most popular place in the canyon to get acquainted with the creek, although I can't recommend it in midsummer. A typical July day brings 1,600 strollers and swimmers, and particularly on weekends, it seems more like a Southern California beach party than any sylvan communion.

The "slide" down a natural sandstone sluice in the creek is great family fun but not without natural risk.

"We have injuries all the time," a park ranger said.

There's more sedate creek swimming at Grasshopper Point (between Mileposts 376 and 377), just north of uptown Sedona.

There are also civilized pleasures in the canyon. One of Arizona's best dining

Clumps of sedges and smooth, black rocks form a striking scene in Oak Creek. Larry Ulrich

experiences is tucked improbably into the forest halfway up the canyon. It's difficult to get a bunk for the night at Garland's Oak Creek Lodge — the regulars book their cabins a year in advance and cancel only under dire circumstances — but dinner reservations are relatively easy to get.

The lodge has been around in some form since the mid-1930s and in the Garland family since 1972, so its traditions may be rooted more deeply than any other commercial enterprise in the Sedona area. Arriving for dinner one evening, I stared at the heroic blaze in the lodge's massive fireplace and felt an echo of that sensation William O. Douglas described: being part of something much bigger than myself, "something great and majestic and wholesome."

Dinner that night was at least great and wholesome:

When You Go

Oak Creek Canyon   Spring and fall are Oak Creek Canyon's best seasons. Summer finds it packed, and some of the cabins close in winter. Some hiking trails are likely to be blocked by snow or ice. Fall color usually peaks around mid-October, although this varies with the elevation.

Slide Rock State Park is open year round. (928) 282-3034. The U.S. Forest Service now requires vehicles to display a Red Rock Pass for parking on National Forest land surrounding Sedona, although no pass is required for travel through the area or when stopping to take a picture. Call the Red Rock Ranger Station at (928) 282-4119 or visit Web site www.redrockcountry.org for details of the conservation program.

Garland's Oak Creek Lodge is open April through mid-November. (928) 282-3343.

Left: Lomaki is one of the ruins at Wupatki National Monument, 60 miles northeast of Sedona. Tom Danielsen Below: These Sinaguan ruins are preserved at Tuzigoot National Monument. Dick Dietrich

tortilla soup sparkling with the flavors of lime and green Anaheim chiles; a salad of red leaf lettuce, jicama, and pomegranate seeds bathed in orange sesame vinaigrette; and a perfect filet mignon lathered with a tart tomatillo sauce. You don't order at Garland's. The kitchen serves whatever they've dreamed up, picked from the garden, or caught. It isn't nouvelle, but it sure isn't cowboy cooking, either. Nor do you pick your dinner companions. You're as likely to be seated at a table with Diane Sawyer (as my tablemates said they were last time) as with . . . me.

Upstream from Garland's, the highway continues to hug the creek for another half-dozen miles, and then it corkscrews out of the canyon onto the Colorado Plateau for the short run through alpine forest to Flagstaff. There's a last stop at the rim, Oak Creek Vista, that offers a spectacular view into the canyon. This, or some place close to it, must have been where Carley Burke, Zane Grey's female lead in *The Call of the Canyon*, first stared into the abyss:

"Carley had never gazed upon a scene like this. Hostile and prejudiced, she yet felt wrung from her an acknowledgment of beauty and grandeur. But wild, violent, savage! Not livable. This insulated rift in the crust of the earth was a gigantic burrow for beasts, perhaps for outlawed men — not for a civilized person."

Carley, of course, lived there happily ever after. And civilization came to the canyon — but not so much so that the wildness entirely vanished.

The Sinagua World

Can a prehistoric experience change a contemporary life? Half an hour at a prehistoric ruin named Honanki, a Hopi word meaning "Bear House", did so for me. I was on an "ancient ruins" Jeep tour out of Sedona with three other visitors and a well-qualified and provocative guide who taught Southwestern prehistory at the college level. When we stopped at Honanki, I first felt a twinge of disappointment. Only a fraction of what had once been an impressive 60-room pueblo remained. But the story line was seductive. Honanki was built around A.D. 1150 and abandoned a little more than a century later, like most of the ruined pueblos around Sedona. Why? Our guide ticked off the standard possibilities: drought, warfare, soil exhaustion. None adequately explained it. He then led us to a petroglyph, a picture etched in the red sandstone cliff overhanging Honanki, and suggested a radical interpretation: It was a comet, which had served as a cosmic sign to begin a great migration.

variations in their art, architecture, and burial practices for archaeologists to classify them as a single, coherent culture. They may have been a composite of others, or they

— very close to the time that Wupatki was built. Its masonry looks like Kayenta Anasazi, and the abandonment of Wupatki began around 1225, just as the Kayenta building boom began at Navajo National Monument, 100 miles farther northeast. Wupatki Pueblo also includes a

Left: A warm spring feeds Montezuma Well, a part of Montezuma Castle National Monument. George H.H. Huey
Below: Visitors can walk by this reconstructed dwelling at Walnut Canyon National Monument. Laurence Parent

I was dubious, and I remain so today. But that moment ignited my curiosity. Over the next six years, I prowled every publicly accessible prehistoric ruin in the Southwest, interviewed scores of archaeologists, and finally wrote an *Arizona Highways* book (*A.D. 1250: Ancient Peoples of the Southwest*) to try to illuminate that shadowy question: What happened to them?

Hundreds of prehistoric pueblos and granaries huddle in the red canyons around Sedona. Hundreds more are strewn across the Verde Valley, to the south, and there are literally thousands on the Colorado Plateau to the north. Those closest to Sedona were built by the Sinagua people, who confound modern archaeologists. "Sinagua," a Spanish compound that means "without water," describes only their environment — average annual rainfall at their pueblo sites today ranges from 7 to 20 inches. But there were too many

might have been a medley of people not even unified by a common language.

You meet the Sinagua identity crisis head-on at Wupatki National Monument, 60 miles northeast of Sedona. This chilly, austere desert in the rain shadow of the San Francisco Peaks seems an unlikely harbor for any civilization, let alone one that didn't have the technology to move water and food over long distances. But there are about 2,000 Sinagua ruins sprinkled around Wupatki, and it appears to have been an important prehistoric crossroads.

The national monument shows off the Sinagua culture at its most ambitious with Wupatki Pueblo, a 100-room apartment building behind the visitors center. But is it really Sinaguan? To anyone versed in prehistoric Southwestern architecture, the building's form clearly echoes the "great houses" of New Mexico's Chaco Canyon, which began to be abandoned around A.D. 1130

sunken ball court, which suggests that its inhabitants, whoever they were, had plugged into the ceremonial sports conference of the desert Hohokam people around present-day Phoenix. "Whoever they were..." sounds like an eternal qualifier for the people of Wupatki.

But their architecture was, and is, breathtaking. Every time I visit Sedona, I schedule one morning's departure for 4 or 5 o'clock, depending on the season, so I can arrive at Wupatki's Wukoki Ruin for sunrise. This little building, which probably sheltered an extended Sinagua family, buds from a sandstone outcropping with such organic grace that it is as if God had turned to the human masons and said, "I'm tired of working on this rock; you finish the job." At sunrise or sunset, the red

Wukoki probably housed an extended Sinaguan family.
Laurence Parent

desert is bathed in fire colors, there is never anyone else around, and I am wrapped in the counterpoint of profound beauty and immense loneliness. It is tempting to imagine that the Sinaguans felt this way 800 years ago.

Thirty miles to the south, outside the rain shadow of the mountains, the northern Sinagua also occupied Walnut Canyon, a forested 385-foot-deep furrow in the ponderosa forest. Though not as dramatic as the Wupatki ruins, some of the 300 dwellings

in Walnut Canyon National Monument have been stabilized and repaired. Visitors can peer inside for a valuable demonstration of how confining, cold and dark Sinagua apartments actually were.

The southern branch of the Sinagua culture is preserved at a Forest Service rock art site and at two other National Monuments in the Verde Valley.

A spectacular clutter of 1,032 petroglyphs blankets a small sandstone bluff at the V Bar V, a working ranch until

Sinagua people tucked this three-story dwelling — misleadingly named Montezuma Castle — into an alcove in a limestone cliff.
George H.H. Huey

When You Go

The Sinagua World   It isn't possible to design a single day trip to explore the Sinagua world — it's too big. Split it into northern and southern Sinagua — which more and more archaeologists are inclined to do.

Northern Sinagua: You might not think you want to do this, but consider leaving Sedona at 4 or 5 A.M. for the 2-hour drive into Sunset Crater Volcano-Wupatki National Monuments. From Flagstaff, take U.S. Route 89 north for 12 miles. Turn right at the sign marking the entrance. The park is open sunrise to sunset, and the turnoff to Wukoki Ruin is easy to find, even in the first strain of morning light. It's the paved spur to the right 21 miles from the south park entrance. (928) 679-2365.

Returning to Flagstaff, turn east on Interstate 40 to Walnut Canyon national monument. The three-quarter mile trail to the ruins descends and climbs 185 feet and is worth the moderate effort. (928) 526-3367.

For the afternoon, visit the Museum of Northern Arizona 3 miles northwest of Flagstaff on Fort Valley Road (U.S. Route 180). The permanent exhibit on the native peoples of the region, including the Sinagua, is thorough and fascinating. (928) 774-5213.

Southern Sinagua: Palatki and Honanki, two small ruins near Sedona, are administered by the National Forest Service. Take State Route 89A west 9.5 miles from the "Y" intersection with State Route 179 in Sedona. Turn right on Forest Service Road 525, drive 6 miles to where Forest Service Road 795 branches to the right, and take FR 795 2 miles to its dead end. The trail to the north leads 0.2 mile to Palatki, and the trail to the west leads 0.2 mile to a petroglyph site. For Honanki, continue on FR 525 another 3.2 miles beyond its intersection with FR 795. For more information, call Coconino National Forest Red Rock Ranger District, (928) 282-4119.

After Palatki and Honanki, return to State 89A and continue south to Tuzigoot National Monument, (928) 634-5564. Montezuma Castle National Monument is located near Camp Verde, 3 miles east of Interstate 17. Use Exit Number 289 and follow the signs. (928) 567-3322, ext. 21. To find the V Bar V petroglyph site, take State 179 to its intersection with I-17 and continue 3 miles east on Forest Service Road 618. Open Friday through Monday only. (928) 282-4119.

Archaeological Etiquette and Felonies   The Arizona Antiquities Act of 1960 made it a felony to remove or damage prehistoric artifacts from state-owned land. The U.S. Archaeological Resources Protection Act of 1979 protects artifacts on federal land. A prehistoric potsherd stashed in someone's desk drawer is meaningless; that same fragment left in the context where it fell a millennium past might someday help archaeologists fill in some blanks in our understanding of the ancient peoples of the Southwest. Take only photographs; leave only footprints.

1994. The Forest Service now welcomes the public to view the bewildering profusion of snakes, toads, mammals, sun signs, mazes, human figures, and possible migration routes — one of the Southwest's densest rock art sites.

Montezuma Castle was badly misnamed by U.S. Army scouts who stumbled across it in the 1860s. It was built at least two centuries before the reign of the final Aztec emperor, who never came within a thousand miles of Arizona. But it is a remarkably ambitious structure, some 65 rooms filling a deep alcove in a limestone cliff. And it is an excellent example of passive solar engineering. Its concave facade is designed to fetch the winter sunlight and fend off the midday summer sun. Whoever they were, the Sinagua knew something about architecture.

Tuzigoot, too, is a marvelous piece of work, anticipating by 800 years Frank Lloyd Wright's dictum that "No house should ever be on any hill . . . it should be of the hill." The village follows the contours of a 100-foot-high ridge overlooking the Verde River with such consummate grace that the hill would seem unfinished today without it. It seems unlikely, however, that the Tuzigootians had aesthetics in mind. It would have been safe from the Verde's periodic flooding, and the high ground provided wary people a natural lookout.

An interesting footnote is that the people of Tuzigoot apparently became more wary over time. At some point, ground-floor doorways were sealed, leaving only rooftop

entrances. By the time the pueblo was abandoned around 1425, there was just one outside doorway for 77 ground-floor rooms.

This and a few other tantalizing clues caused me to spend a good part of six years panning for evidence of the prehistoric war that either dispersed or killed off not only the Sinagua, but also every other major culture in Arizona between 1250 and 1450. But there was no great war. There just came to be too many people for a fragile environment to support — a disarmingly simple explanation that reverberates around the increasingly crowded red rocks today.

Jerome

"The Wickedest Town in America," hissed the *New York Sun* in 1903. Not about its hometown, but about tiny Jerome, Arizona, a rickety mountainside village 2,000 miles west of New York and a hundred miles north of Phoenix. Not only was the place rife with boozing, wenching, brawling, and gambling, reported the newspaper; it also was ugly, noisy, congested, and polluted. The best thing that could happen to Jerome, the *Sun* snarled, would be a nice, big, citywide fire.

The *Sun's* tirade was reprinted locally and was greeted with predictable howls of outrage. Read it today, and it seems funny and ironic — New York, the pot, scolding this harmless kettle of a town for its pollution and immorality. But the writer was not far wrong. Jerome, in its mining years, was truly a hell of a place to live and work.

"We have a tendency to romanticize mining and mining

towns here in the West," said Arizona historian James W. Byrkit, who grew up three miles downslope in Clarkdale. "But there was never anything romantic about Jerome."

Nevertheless, the romanticism is in full bloom today. Jerome has become a major attraction, an essential stop for tour buses on the Prescott-Sedona-Grand Canyon swing. And there are good reasons to come here, though not all the locals appreciate the throngs in the streets.

Jerome was born with a copper mining claim in 1876. A rudimentary mining camp quickly sprang up around the first shafts. In 1883, the United Verde Copper Company built the camp's first smelter. Ten years later, a narrow-gauge railway replaced the 20-mule freight wagons that had been groaning over 7,743-foot Mingus Mountain. Jerome then was ready for civilization of a sort.

But not since the Ancestral Puebloan cliff dwellings of 1250 had an American settlement been so improbably located. Jerome's Victorian houses and hotels were stitched onto the side of Mingus Mountain, every building site a 10- or 20-percent grade. Main Street's switchbacks resembled a snake doubled up with stomach gas. In 1899, a Phoenix newspaperman noted that "your neighbor to the rear, in Jerome, can't look into your back windows, although he can look down your kitchen chimney from his front porch."

Still, by 1900, Jerome claimed 2,681 residents, which made it the fifth largest town in Arizona Territory. It was no

longer a mining camp, but a place with at least the veneer of civilization. The Montana Hotel, which opened that year, was a handsome, carefully detailed, four-story Georgian Revival building that would have been quite at home in Boston. Its architecture helped convince inhabitants and visitors that Jerome was for real. By this time, the mines were throwing off enough copper, silver, and gold that the town was attracting some serious cigars.

But the high style was an illusion. Jerome wasn't stable or sophisticated. It was raw, tough, precarious, dangerous, and yes, wicked.

Spindly wooden buildings stacked practically atop one another made Jerome a firetrap. Devastating blazes swept through town in 1894, '97, '98, '99, 1902, '07, '11, and '15 — the last fire claiming the grand Montana. There also were floods, mudslides, epidemics of smallpox and scarlet fever, street violence, and, most of all, the mine work itself. Hear Byrkit again. It was never romantic. Between 1895 and 1935, despite the claims of United Verde executives that "everything possible was being done [for safety]," about 150 miners lost their lives in the man-made bowels of Mingus Mountain. This was the true wickedness of Jerome.

The ore vein was essentially vertical, and the main shaft plunged 4,650 feet into the mountain. At the bottom was the foyer of hell.

Byrkit, son of a mine executive, recalled a boyhood visit in the 1940s: "The miners were in rubber boots, working in water about a foot deep. It was humid and very, very hot — I would guess over 100°. They could work only 20 minutes without a rest."

Prostitution was a major industry in Jerome, maybe second only to mining. It was intermittently legal and regulated, with the "girls" required to report for biweekly medical exams.

Fires and mudslides destroyed most of Jerome's original buildings, but the entire town is a historic landmark.
George H.H. Huey

There were opium dens, gambling houses, and scores of saloons, occasionally featuring bands or vaudeville acts. There was a chronic shortage of rooms for the miners, so they rented rooms and bunks in shifts. A miners' circadian rhythm evolved: eight hours working, eight hours drinking, eight hours sleeping, the clock segments interchangeable depending on which shift one spent underground.

Jerome was a goulash of ethnicity, far more interesting than the big towns of Phoenix and Tucson at the time. In 1918, the United Verde issued a nationality report on its Jerome employees, revealing that those born on U.S. soil were a minority. There were 401 Mexicans, 393 Americans, 96 Slavs, 68 Spaniards, 60 Austrians, 57 Italians, 53 Irish, and 32 Serbs. Ethnic tensions were not unknown, but down in the mine, at least, the men worked as brothers. Their lives depended on it.

For a boomtown, Jerome had an unusually long life. With the end of World War I and the decline in demand for copper jackets for bullets, the mining went on, but at a slowing pace. Finally, in 1953, the mine shut down. In 77 years, Mingus Mountain had given up an estimated $1 billion in copper, gold, silver, zinc, and lead.

In a universe driven by logic and not sentiment, Jerome would have died right then. There never had been any industry except for mining, and there appeared to be no reason for anyone to stay. The population evaporated to fewer than 50. One evening the superintendent of Tuzigoot National Monument came to a town meeting and informed the last stalwarts that visitors seemed more interested in Jerome's history than Tuzigoot's prehistory. A handful of people then formed the Jerome Historical Society, believing that the story of this colorful, wicked town was worth preserving.

Jerome's revival began tentatively around 1970. A few people who had lived in the town during the mining years returned to retire. Then a few bohemians and artists discovered the preposterously low cost of living and rim-of-the-world views off Mingus Mountain.

Nancy Smith, an unofficial town historian, recalled coming to Jerome in 1972: "The younger people lived in apartment buildings (formerly miners' boarding houses), with an agreement that we would take care of minor things and not bother the owners with a lot of complaints. These people didn't need a lot of money to live, and they provided an inexpensive labor force for restoration. My situation was typical. I moved into an attic apartment with one of the most fantastic views in the world — and it was $25 a month."

Jerome today is Arizona's oddest town. The population is still tiny — just 329 in the 2000 census. Most of the 1890-1915 buildings are gone, victims of the fires or mudslides. But there are still about 300 historic houses and commercial buildings standing (the whole town resides on the National Register of Historic Places). Many have been restored; a few still stand as silent ruins. The raffish, improvisatory nature of the architecture, a slapdash echo of the Victorian era, meshes perfectly with the dreamers who've resettled the town. Rusty mine implements and splintery wagon wheels informally decorate gardens; Volkswagen microbuses hang around with bumper stickers such as "My Karma Just Ran Over Your Dogma." The prime fund-raising venue for historic preservation is an outhouse planted in the ruins of the 1901 Bartlett

Hotel; visitors are cordially invited to pitch their coins at the hole. Externally, at least, Jerome is an outdoor museum of the sixties.

But it's also a haven for serious artists. For 25 years Robin Anderson and Margo Mandette have leased the defunct high school, built in 1911, as their studio and gallery. They came from New York looking for peace, quiet, and space, and found all three. Anderson does Verde River landscapes, large-scale figure sculptures and challenging conceptual portraits. Mandette ranges from rustic pottery through cartoonlike cat paintings to swirling abstractions. "We have 20,000 square feet here," said Anderson. "No one could afford anything like this in New York. This building is enabling all this creativity."

More than a dozen galleries operate in Jerome, and the ratio of art to kitsch has tilted more toward art over the last few years. Tracy Weisel's thoroughly sophisticated Raku Gallery looks like it could have been transplanted from San Francisco. But there's still more eccentricity and lower prices in Jerome than in Sedona. The overhead is lower, so the risk-taking can be higher.

Another turn of eccentricity is the Holy Family Catholic Church, whose painted wooden neo-Gothic reredos has a folk-art charm about it. The story behind the church's restoration is classic Jerome. When the Rev. Juan Atucha, the last full-time pastor,

Choices for shoppers in Jerome are eclectic and eccentric.
Tom Bean

died in 1979, parishioners found about $60,000 in change and small bills stashed about the rectory and church. He'd been hoarding it, apparently, for 30 years. Thanks to his odd habit, the church was restored the following year.

Jerome is losing population again (a decline of 18 percent between 1990 and 2000), but for visitors, the experience has never been better. Two hotels are now open — the restored 1898 Connor and the Jerome Grand, a 1927 hospital that reopened as a hotel in 1996. An overnight stay in Jerome is a treat — not because of the night life, which is nonexistent except for occasional live music in one bar; but for the opportunity to wander the silent streets early in the morning, watching dawn probe the ruins of the Bartlett and surprising a javelina foraging in an overgrown garden. At such a moment Jerome is undebatably romantic.

The Verde Valley

Downslope from Jerome, the Verde River glides through sandstone canyons and forests of sycamore and cottonwood trees en route to an eventual rendezvous with the Salt River east of Phoenix. The towns strung through the valley — Clarkdale, Cottonwood, Cornville, Camp Verde — are beginning to nourish arts communities of their own as Sedona becomes more expensive.

Recreation and history are offered in three state parks. Dead

The Verde River nourishes towns such as Clarkdale and stands of cottonwoods and sycamores alike.
Bob & Suzanne Clemenz

78

Top: This lagoon is a central feature
at Dead Horse Ranch State Park.
George Stocking
Above: The Verde Canyon Railroad
ventures into a canyon loaded with
scenery and wildlife. Tom Johnson
Left: Fort Verde State Historic Park
traces its origins to a fort built in 1871.
Richard Maack

Horse Ranch's 320 riparian acres provide an engaging venue for birding, picnicking, or canoeing along the Verde River. Jerome State Historic Park, housed in an 8,000-square-foot mansion built in 1916 by mine magnate James S. Douglas, displays Mingus Mountain's mining history. Fort Verde State Historic Park is a U.S. Army fort built in 1871 to subdue the Yavapai and Apache, who were troubling the Anglos newly arrived to farm and ranch the valley. One visitor's comment in the guest register seemed to say it all: "A good exhibit on a sad part of American history."

One of the valley's most popular captivations is the Verde Canyon Railroad, which carries about 90,000 passengers a year on a 12-mile-an-hour dawdle from Clarkdale to the nearly nonexistent settlement of Perkinsville and back. One of its chief attractions is nostalgia: On every excursion there's a grandparent who used to ride the train and a grandchild who's never before been aboard one. The other is scenery. The train rumbles through woodlands, where the cottonwood canopies span 50 feet, and then into a canyon where the rufous sandstone walls eventually tower 700 feet above the train. Great blue herons and golden and bald eagles winter in the canyon, joining year-round resident javelinas, beavers, river otters, mountain lions, bobcats, black bears, and wild turkeys. There's no other way to see this; the railroad is the only road into the canyon.

A snowy Mingus Mountain presides over Cottonwood, basking in the the ample sunshine of the Verde Valley.
Bob & Suzanne Clemenz

A prehistoric civilization, a painful chapter in the building of America, a wicked Victorian mining town, a slow train into a vanished past — the Verde Valley seems so young, and yet a thousand years of human history lies right on its surface, taking in the abundant sun.

When You Go

Jerome And The Verde Valley   Most of the valley lies at an elevation of 3,300 to 3,500 feet —1,000 feet lower than Sedona — so expect a hot summer and a mild winter.

For tourist information: Cottonwood-Verde Valley Chamber of Commerce, (928) 634-7593. Jerome Chamber of Commerce, (928) 634-2900. Camp Verde Chamber of Commerce, (928) 567-9294. Jerome has a Web site: http://www.sedona.net/jerome/

Dead Horse Ranch State Park, (928) 634-5283. Fort Verde State Historic Park, (928) 567-3275. Jerome State Historic Park, (928) 634-5381. The Arizona State Parks Web site: www.pr.state.az.us

The Verde Canyon Railroad offers excursions leaving Clarkdale at 1 P.M. most days of the week, depending on season. Saturday night starlight rides run from May through August. Reservations required for all excursions. Call (800) 293-7245 or (928) 639-0010 for a schedule or visit their Web site: www.verdecanyonrr.com.

CHAPTER FIVE

Farther Out

Excursions to the Grand Canyon,
Mogollon Rim, and Navajoland

With the rainbow hanging high on the ends of your wings, come to us soaring.
— NAVAJO NIGHT CHANT
(1902 English translation)

These excursions are overnighters, because they encompass too many miles and too many sensations to fold into a single day. The Grand Canyon is only 120 miles away, but most of those miles are congested, so figure three hours each way.

Grand Canyon

Bruce Babbitt, a former Arizona governor and Secretary of the Interior, told this story in a Grand Canyon anthology he edited years ago: He was standing near a clump of tourists at the South Rim as a world-class sunset ripened over the Canyon. One of them snapped a Polaroid, and the rest all turned away from the sky to watch the image of it develop.

The Canyon and its skies are so overwhelming, so far outside the range of other human experience, that our senses at first refuse to comprehend.

Which is the prime argument for spending serious time with the Canyon — hiking it, rafting it, photographing it, sitting on the Rim in quiet meditation at sunrise or sunset.

Destination, Grand Canyon. The itinerary of many Sedona visitors takes them there, to the Rim or down into it.
Top: Rafters plunge through Hermit Rapid on the Colorado River.
Kerrick James

Above: From Yaki Point on the South Rim, sunset fires the emotions of watchers.
Tom Bean
Opposite page:
Sunrise bathes Cape Royal on the North Rim.
George Stocking

One needs "To step off the brink," as Babbitt wrote, "and to get personally involved in the demanding reality of the Canyon."

A two-day excursion to the South Rim from Sedona could conveniently take in the Museum of Northern Arizona en route, a full afternoon and evening on the South Rim, and an all-day hike into the Canyon the following day on Bright Angel or South Kaibab trail. Very strong hikers can make the trip to the Canyon floor and back in a day (elevation gain 4,600 feet), but the return to Sedona would call for a designated driver.

Mogollon Rim

There are countless places in Arizona where one can go to contemplate the Apache wars, but none is more dramatically scenic than a little-known gravel logging road that closely follows the trail that Gen. George Crook blazed along the edge of the Mogollon Rim some 130 years ago.

It was here on an August afternoon in 1872 that Crook and his men were scouting the terrain and blazing a supply trail when the Tonto Apaches introduced themselves with a blizzard of arrows. The soldiers scrambled for cover, returned fire, and most of the Apaches melted back into the forest. Two of them, trapped by the soldiers right on the lip of the 2,000-foot escarpment, fired

The Apache wars burned the Mogollon Rim into Arizona's history. Dick Dietrich

85

their last arrows in defiance, then leaped over the rim, apparently choosing suicide over capture. When Crook's men rushed over, they saw two Apaches leaping "like mountain sheep" from rock to rock. Because of encounters like this, Crook developed a profound respect for the people he was under orders to subdue.

It's a 215-mile round trip from Sedona to the scenic drive along Forest Service Road 300, which parallels the rim. The gravel road is fine for passenger cars in dry weather but is usually closed to all traffic in winter. From Sedona, take State Route 179 and Interstate 17 to Camp Verde and drive east on State Route 260 to State Route 87. Turn left (north) and drive a few miles for the turnoff for FR 300 — on the right, just beyond

Milepost 281. The forest road intersects State 260 a little more than 30 miles east of Payson. Montezuma Castle, Fort Verde State Historic Park, and Tonto Natural Bridge State Park all lie conveniently along the loop.

Navajoland

The Navajo Reservation, or Navajo Nation, is almost twice the size of Switzerland and at least as resplendent in natural and cultural attractions. A three-day loop from Sedona would cover about 550 miles, taking in the possibilities of Navajo National Monument, Monument Valley, Canyon de Chelly, Hubbell Trading Post, and as a bonus, nearby Petrified Forest National Park. Another premium on this excursion is inevitable contact with the

Above: Betatakin, a 135-room dwelling built by the Ancestral Pueblo people, seems to flow out of the cliff at Navajo National Monument.
Tom Danielsen
Opposite page: As the sun rises, the shadows of stone monoliths dance across Monument Valley. This view looks north from Hunts Mesa.
Robert G. McDonald

Diné, "the People," as the Navajos call themselves. I have always found Navajos to be wonderfully direct and engaging. If you approach with genuine interest and respect, Navajos will talk with you openly.

Navajo National Monument includes the most extravagant and best-preserved Ancestral Puebloan ruins in Arizona, but they are open only in summer and require both advance planning and sweat

FARTHER OUT

Right: White House Ruin
remains a timeless memorial
to prehistoric people who
lived in Canyon de Chelly.
Dick Dietrich
Below: The old ways are still
a way of life in Monument Valley:
A lone Navajo woman tends sheep
and a rider and members of his
family drive a flock across the sand.
Both by Edward McCain

to see. Betatakin is a 5-mile round-trip hike; Keet Seel is 17 miles round trip by foot. Both are well worth the effort.

Canyon de Chelly National Monument secretes about 400 Ancestral Puebloan ruins in an awesomely beautiful canyon system shaped like a giant bird's gnarled footprint. Only one ruin, the White House, is accessible without a guide. Very highly recommended: Half- or all-day vehicle or horseback tours of the canyon floor with Navajo guides. Paved roads overlooking the south rim (36 miles round trip) and north rim (34 miles) are also well worth the time.

Monument Valley is a Navajo tribal park, not U.S. government property, and it, too, is experienced most intimately with a native guide. Visitors on their own may drive the park's 17-mile loop, but do not venture off-road to hike, picnic, or camp without a guide.

Hubbell Trading Post at Ganado was founded in 1876 and is still open for business as a privately owned National Historic Site. Bargains in Navajo rugs are now memories as

ancient as nickel Cokes, but the quantity and quality of Hubbell's selection is staggering, and worth a special stop, if only for dreaming.

Petrified Forest National Park is famous, of course, for its unique landscape litter of 225-million-year-old logs. The park's prehistoric Puebloan ruins are modest, but an unadvertised special is one of the most concentrated petroglyph collections in Arizona. Walk south across the mesa from the

Puerco Ruin and look among the rocks at the foot of the slope.

"OBVIOUS ARIZONA," Vladimir Nabokov called it in *Lolita*, this land of polychrome earth, yawning blue canyons, and sculpted red rocks. The images are obvious because they're so familiar; in the world's eyes, they are Arizona. But the land continues to make promises to the human spirit and to reward a lifetime's

Right: Hubbell Trading Post has been serving the Navajo people as supplier, banker, and buyer of their goods for more than 120 years.
Jerry Jacka
Opposite page: Petrified logs form a unique landscape in Jasper Forest in the Petrified Forest National Park.
Larry Ulrich

acquaintance. The closing lines of the Navajo Night Chant capture the essence of this relationship:

With beauty before me,
I walk.
With beauty behind me,
I walk.
With beauty below me,
I walk.
With beauty above me,
I walk.
With beauty all around me,
I walk.
It is finished in beauty.

When You Go

For general Grand Canyon National Park information, call (928) 638-7888. For accommodations inside the park, call (928) 638-2401. There are also motels at Tusayan, 10 miles from the South Rim visitors center.

For information regarding the suggested Mogollon Rim excursion: Montezuma Castle National Monument, (928) 567-3322. Fort Verde State Historic Park, (928) 567-3275. Tonto Natural Bridge State Park, (928) 476-4202. Rim Country Regional Chamber of Commerce, (928) 474-4515 or (800) 6-PAYSON (672-9766).

For general inquiries about traveling on the Navajo Reservation, call the Navajo Nation Tourism Department at Tribal Headquarters in Window Rock, (928) 871-6436. Navajo National Monument, (928) 672-2700. Monument Valley, (435) 727-5870. Canyon de Chelly National Monument, (928) 674-5500. Hubbell Trading Post National Historic Site, (928) 755-3254. Petrified Forest National Park, (928) 524-6228.

These formations and ridgeline identify Bear Wallow Canyon, which runs along a portion of Schnebly Hill Road. Steve Bruno
Following pages 94 and 95:
This view is from the trail leading up Wilson Mountain just north of Sedona. Ship Rock is at left.
Larry Lindahl

Camel Head Rock literally
glows in the setting sun
after a storm. Tom Bean